Southern Living®
ALL-TIME FAVORITE
LOW-FAT
RECIPES

Southern Living®

ALL-TIME FAVORITE
LOW-FAT
RECIPES

Compiled and Edited by
Jean Wickstrom Liles

Oxmoor House®

Copyright 1996 by Oxmoor House, Inc.
Book Division of Southern Progress Corporation
P.O. Box 2463, Birmingham, Alabama 35201

Library of Congress Catalog Number: 95-74599
Hardcover ISBN: 0-8487-2230-2
Softcover ISBN: 0-8487-2223-X
Manufactured in the United States of America
First Printing 1996

Editor-in-Chief: Nancy Fitzpatrick Wyatt
Editorial Director, Special Interest Publications: Ann H. Harvey
Senior Foods Editor: Susan Carlisle Payne
Senior Editor, Editorial Services: Olivia Kindig Wells
Art Director: James Boone

Southern Living® ALL-TIME FAVORITE LOW-FAT RECIPES

Menu and Recipe Consultant: Jean Wickstrom Liles
Assistant Editor: Kelly Hooper Troiano
Copy Editor: Jane Phares
Editorial Assistant: Valorie J. Cooper
Indexer: Mary Ann Laurens
Concept Designer: Melissa Jones Clark
Designer: Rita Yerby
Senior Photographers: Jim Bathie; Charles Walton IV, *Southern Living* magazine
Photographers: Ralph Anderson; Tina Evans, J. Savage Gibson, Sylvia Martin, *Southern Living* magazine
Senior Photo Stylists: Kay E. Clarke; Leslie Byars Simpson, *Southern Living* magazine
Photo Stylists: Virginia R. Cravens; Ashley J. Wyatt, *Southern Living* magazine
Production and Distribution Director: Phillip Lee
Associate Production Managers: Theresa L. Beste, Vanessa D. Cobbs
Production Coordinator: Marianne Jordan Wilson
Production Assistant: Valerie L. Heard

Our appreciation to the editorial staff of *Southern Living* magazine and to the Southern Progress Corporation library staff for their contributions to this volume.

Cover: Black Forest Cheesecake (recipe on page 43)
Page 1: Crab Cakes (recipe on page 58)
Page 2: Shrimp-and-Rice Salad (recipe on page 118)

Contents

Low-Fat Basics

Low-fat eating isn't just for people who are trying to lose weight. Today everyone can benefit from keeping dietary fat to 30 percent or less of total daily calories. Research studies show that decreasing your fat intake can also reduce risks of heart disease, diabetes, and some types of cancer.

How Much Fat?

The current dietary recommendation to reduce fat intake to no more than 30 percent of total calories refers to the fat intake for the entire day. If you have a high-fat item at one meal, you can balance it with low-fat choices for the rest of the day and still remain within the recommended percentage. The goal of fat reduction need not be to eliminate fat from the diet. Some fat is necessary each day to transport fat-soluble vitamins and maintain other normal body functions.

To achieve a diet with 30 percent or less of total calories from fat, first establish a fat budget for the day based on the total number of daily calories needed. Estimate your daily calorie requirements by multiplying your current weight by 15. (This is only a rough guide because calorie requirements vary by age, body size, and level of physical activity.) Once you determine your personal daily calorie requirement, use the Daily Fat Limits chart (right) to figure the maximum amount of fat grams allowed each day for you to stay within the recommended percentages. For example, if you are consuming 1,800 calories per day, you should eat no more than 60 grams of fat per day.

Daily Fat Limits		
Calories Per Day	30 Percent of Calories	Grams of Fat
1,200	360	40
1,500	450	50
1,800	540	60
2,000	600	67
2,200	660	73
2,500	750	83
2,800	840	93

Nutritional Analysis

Southern Living All-Time Favorite Low-Fat Recipes has a realistic approach to trimming fat from your diet. While each recipe has been kitchen-tested by a staff of home economists, registered dietitians have determined the nutritional information using a computer system that analyzes each ingredient.

The nutrient grid following each recipe includes calories per serving and the percentage of calories from fat. Also, the grid lists the grams of total fat, saturated fat, protein, and carbohydrate, and the milligrams of cholesterol and sodium per serving. The nutrient values are as accurate as possible and are based on these assumptions:

• All meats are trimmed of fat and skin before cooking.

• When the recipe calls for cooked pasta, rice, or noodles, the analysis is based on cooking without additional salt or fat.

• Fruits and vegetables listed in the ingredients are not peeled unless specified.

• When a range is given for an ingredient, the lesser amount is calculated.

• A percentage of alcohol calories evaporates when heated; this reduction is reflected in the calculations.

• When a marinade is used, only the amount of marinade absorbed is calculated.

• Garnishes and optional ingredients are not calculated.

Low-Fat Cooking Tips

These cooking techniques are basic to low-fat cooking. Apply these techniques to your own recipes to turn high-fat standbys into healthy favorites.

• Buy only the leanest cuts of beef, pork, lamb, and veal. Select cuts such as beef tenderloin, beef round, beef sirloin, pork tenderloin, pork loin chops, leg of lamb, lamb loin chops, and veal cutlets. Trim meat of all visible fat before cooking.

• Trim fat and remove the skin of chicken and turkey before or after cooking.

• Brown ground meat in a nonstick skillet or in a skillet coated with vegetable cooking spray. In addition to lean ground beef, try ground turkey breast or ground chicken breast.

After cooking the meat, place it in a colander to drain excess fat. To further reduce the fat, pat the cooked meat dry with paper towels after draining, and wipe drippings from the skillet with a paper towel before continuing to cook.

Draining meat in a colander

• Roast meats and poultry on a rack in a broiler pan so fat can drip away. For easy cleanup, coat broiler pan with vegetable cooking spray before cooking.

• Marinate lean meats, fish, and poultry in fat-free or low-fat marinades to enhance their flavors. Reduce or omit oil from marinade recipes by substituting water or broth. Other low-fat ingredients for marinades include citrus juices, wines, and flavored vinegars.

• Cook pasta, rice, grains, and green and starchy vegetables with little or no added fat. Steaming, sautéing, and stir-frying are best for cooking vegetables because these require a minimum of fat while preserving nutrients. Use a nonstick skillet or wok or a skillet coated with vegetable cooking spray for sautéing and stir-frying.

Sautéing in a nonstick skillet

• Coat baking dishes, pans, and casseroles with vegetable cooking spray instead of butter, oil, or shortening. To add more flavor to foods, use olive oil-flavored or butter-flavored cooking spray.

• Make soups, stews, stocks, or broths ahead of time, and chill overnight in the refrigerator. After the soup has chilled, skim off the hardened fat with a spoon, and discard the fat; then reheat.

If there is no time to chill the soup, skim off as much fat as possible, and add several ice cubes to the warm liquid. The fat will cling to the ice cubes, which can then be removed and discarded.

Skimming fat from soup

• Use herbs, spices, and salt-free seasoning blends to flavor vegetables, meats, fish, and poultry. Citrus juices, flavored vinegars, and wines can also help bring out the natural flavor of foods. To substitute dried herbs for fresh, use approximately one-third of the fresh amount.

• Substitute skim milk when a recipe calls for cream or whole milk. And if the recipe doesn't look creamy enough, add nonfat dry milk 1 table-spoon at a time until desired consistency is reached.

• Use whipped evaporated skimmed milk in place of fat-laden whipping cream or whipped topping mixes. Place evaporated skimmed milk in a mixing bowl; place the mixing

bowl and the beaters in the freezer for 30 minutes or until small ice crystals form around the top of the bowl. Remove the bowl and the beaters from the freezer, and beat milk at high speed until soft peaks form.

Whipping evaporated skimmed milk

• Use reduced-fat cheese and nonfat sour cream and yogurt. Since many of the reduced-fat cheeses are still over 50 percent fat, try to substitute a strong-flavored cheese and use less of it. You'll get the cheese flavor without all the fat.

When cooking with yogurt, keep temperature low and heating time short to prevent separation.

• Decrease butter, margarine, vegetable oil, and shortening. When fat is decreased, you may need to add a liquid such as water, fruit juice, or skim milk to make up for moisture loss.

Although margarine and vegetable oils contain about the same number of fat grams and calories as butter, they are lower in saturated fat and cholesterol.

Use reduced-fat margarine for some recipes but not baked

goods unless specified; the water that is whipped into reduced-calorie margarine may cause sogginess.

• Use egg whites or an egg substitute in place of whole eggs. Instead of one whole egg, use two egg whites or one-fourth cup egg substitute. Egg whites and egg substitutes should be cooked over low heat, or they will toughen and become dry.

Low-Fat Cooking Methods

Low fat doesn't have to mean low flavor. These cooking methods will help you achieve the fullest flavor possible while keeping the fat content low.

• *Bake or roast.* Cooking in an oven where the food is surrounded by dry heat is known as baking or roasting. Baked meats and poultry are generally covered and may have liquid added to help keep them moist. Roasted meats and poultry are cooked uncovered, without the addition of liquid, until they have a well-browned exterior and moist interior.

To prevent lean meats from drying out, marinate in a low-fat marinade before roasting, or baste with a low-fat liquid while cooking. Baking works well for lean meats and poultry, and roasting requires fairly tender cuts of meat or poultry.

• *Braise or stew.* Cooking food slowly in a small amount of liquid in a tightly covered pot is known as braising or stewing. Use either of these methods to develop the flavor of the food and to tenderize tough cuts of meat. Unlike stewing, braising requires that meat be browned before it is covered with liquid and simmered. Coat the pan with cooking spray or a small amount of vegetable oil when browning meat. Stewing usually requires more liquid than braising and uses smaller pieces of meat.

• *Broil or grill.* Cooking food directly over or under a heat source is known as broiling or grilling. The cooking temperature is regulated by the distance between the food and the heat source. To broil foods, place meats, fish, and poultry on a rack in a broiler pan to allow fat to drip away from the food.

When grilling, coat the grill rack with vegetable cooking spray before placing over the coals. The cooking spray helps keep the food from sticking.

Broiling fish on a rack

• *Oven-fry.* Baking foods on a rack to give all sides equal exposure to the heat is known as oven-frying. The food is often breaded, and the result is a crisp outer coating and juicy interior similar to that of deep-fat fried foods. Oven-frying is a low-fat cooking method often used for pork chops, chicken, and fish.

• *Poach.* Cooking food gently in water or other liquid held just below the boiling point is called poaching. No added fat is required, and the food retains its flavor, shape, and texture. Poultry, firm fish, and firm fruits such as pears and apples are examples of foods suitable for poaching.

Poaching chicken in seasoned liquid

• *Steam.* Cooking food over, not in, boiling water is called steaming. Food is placed on a rack or in a steamer basket and covered. If you don't have a steamer basket, you can place a colander or strainer in a large saucepan and cover it tightly. Food can also be steamed in the oven without any liquid in a parchment paper package (*en papillote*) or in a package made from heavy-duty aluminum foil.

No added fat is needed for steaming, and the food retains its shape, texture, and flavor. Fish, shellfish, poultry, and vegetables are ideal foods for steaming.

Steaming vegetables in a steamer basket

• *Stir-fry or sauté.* Cooking food quickly in a wok or skillet over high heat in a small amount of fat is known as stir-frying or sautéing. Coating a nonstick skillet or wok with vegetable cooking spray or cooking in a small amount of broth, wine, vinegar, or water can eliminate the need for added fat. The ingredients are stirred in the pan constantly during cooking so that they cook evenly. Because it is deep and has sloping sides, a wok requires less fat than does a skillet.

Low-Fat Cooking Tools
Use these kitchen tools to make low-fat cooking easier.

• A colander or strainer allows you to drain fat from cooked ground meats as well as drain liquid from other foods.

Spoon cooked ground meat into the colander, let the fat drain, and discard fat.

• An egg separator easily separates the low-fat egg white from the higher-fat yolk. It holds the yolk in the saucer and allows the white to slide through the slots.

• A fat-off ladle allows you to skim fat from meat stocks, soups, and stews. When the ladle is lowered into the liquid, the fat flows through slots around the edge of the ladle and collects in the bowl. When the ladle is full, pour off fat from the opposite end.

• A gravy strainer or a fat-separating cup looks like a measuring cup with a spout. The spout, attached near the bottom of the cup, allows liquid to be poured out while the fat floats to the top.

Skimming fat from liquids with a gravy strainer

• Kitchen shears make easy work of trimming excess fat from meats and poultry, cutting fins off fish, cutting poultry into pieces, snipping fresh herbs, and performing a variety of other kitchen tasks.

• Nonstick baking pans, baking sheets, and muffin pans allow baking without having to heavily grease the pan. This decreases the amount of fat.

• A nonstick skillet helps keep fat to a minimum because foods that already contain fat, such as meat and poultry, can be cooked without adding additional fat. And fruits, vegetables, and other foods with almost no fat can be cooked successfully with just a little vegetable cooking spray.

• A steam basket or steamer allows food to cook without the addition of fat. Because the food is not cooked in water, vitamin loss is minimal. Many varieties of steamers are available, from metal baskets to stackable bamboo baskets. A simple rack or folding steam basket that prevents food from touching the water will work for most recipes.

Cooking fresh vegetables in a folding steam basket

• A wire grilling basket prevents tender fish steaks, fillets, and vegetables from falling through the grill rack. To prevent sticking and to aid in cleanup, coat the basket with vegetable cooking spray before adding the food.

• A wok is the favored cooking utensil for stir-frying because its sloping sides allow for even distribution of heat, quick cooking, and the use of very little oil. The traditional wok has a round bottom for cooking over a gas flame. Flat-bottomed woks and stir-fry pans are for cooking on electric cooktops. Nonstick woks and stir-fry pans can eliminate the need for added fat.

Stir-frying fresh vegetables in a wok

• A ruler is helpful for measuring the dimensions and thicknesses of foods that are called for in some recipes.

• Scales help determine portion sizes; this is important because the cooked weight of food will vary from the uncooked weight. Look for a model that has a sturdy base, gives measurements in ounces, and is easy to read and clean.

Appetizers & Beverages

From simple snacks to fancy hors d'oeuvres, these light-and-healthy appetizers are something to cheer about. We've also included tasty sippers that are satisfying yet low in fat and calories.

Skinny Ranch Dip, Pita Chips, Bagel Chips, Sweet Potato Chips

Spiced Pineapple Sparkle, Spicy Virgin Mary, Snack Mix, White Grape Punch

Garbanzo Dip, Chicken Wontons, Baked Wonton Chips, Parmesan Pita Chips

Potato Skin Snack, Mock Black Russian, Whole Wheat Pretzels

Clockwise from top: Festive Crab Dip (page 12), Chicken Wontons (page 19), Apricot-Orange Bread (page 25), and Tortellini with Rosemary-Parmesan Sauce (page 19)

Festive Crab Dip

(pictured on page 11)

1 (4¼-ounce) can lump crabmeat, drained
1 cup nonfat mayonnaise
¼ cup plain nonfat yogurt
¼ cup nonfat sour cream
1 tablespoon chopped fresh parsley
1 tablespoon diced pimiento, drained
1 tablespoon dry sherry
1 teaspoon lemon juice
¼ teaspoon celery seeds
⅛ teaspoon pepper

Combine all ingredients; cover and chill thoroughly. Serve with assorted fresh vegetables. **Yield: 2 cups.**

PER TABLESPOON: 13 CALORIES (7% FROM FAT)
FAT 0.1G (SATURATED FAT 0.0G)
PROTEIN 1.0G CARBOHYDRATE 1.9G
CHOLESTEROL 3MG SODIUM 110MG

Skinny Ranch Dip

1 (24-ounce) carton nonfat cottage cheese
1 (1.1-ounce) envelope reduced-calorie
    Ranch-style salad dressing mix
½ cup skim milk
1 tablespoon white vinegar

Combine all ingredients in container of an electric blender; cover and process until smooth, stopping once to scrape down sides. Serve with assorted fresh vegetables. **Yield: 3 cups.**

PER TABLESPOON: 12 CALORIES (0% FROM FAT)
FAT 0.0G (SATURATED FAT 0.0G)
PROTEIN 1.9G CARBOHYDRATE 1.2G
CHOLESTEROL 1MG SODIUM 117MG

Garbanzo Dip

1 (19-ounce) can chick-peas (garbanzo beans),
    drained
½ cup commercial oil-free Italian dressing
1 tablespoon fresh lemon juice
1 clove garlic

Combine all ingredients in container of an electric blender; cover and process until smooth, stopping once to scrape down sides. Chill. Serve with fresh vegetables. **Yield: 1¾ cups.**

PER TABLESPOON: 23 CALORIES (12% FROM FAT)
FAT 0.3G (SATURATED FAT 0.0G)
PROTEIN 1.1G CARBOHYDRATE 4.1G
CHOLESTEROL 0MG SODIUM 71MG

Mock Guacamole

2 (10½-ounce) cans cut asparagus, drained
1 cup finely chopped tomato
¼ cup finely chopped onion
2 tablespoons lemon juice
1 tablespoon reduced-calorie mayonnaise
½ teaspoon garlic salt
½ teaspoon chili powder
¼ teaspoon hot sauce

Position knife blade in food processor bowl, and add asparagus. Process until smooth, and transfer to a large mixing bowl.

Stir in tomato and remaining ingredients. Place in a paper towel-lined wire-mesh strainer or colander, and let drain 1 hour.

Cover and chill at least 3 hours before serving with fresh vegetables. **Yield: 2 cups.**

PER TABLESPOON: 6 CALORIES (30% FROM FAT)
FAT 0.2G (SATURATED FAT 0.0G)
PROTEIN 0.3G CARBOHYDRATE 0.9G
CHOLESTEROL 0MG SODIUM 63MG

Artichoke-Parmesan Spread

Artichoke-Parmesan Spread

1 cup soft breadcrumbs
1 cup nonfat mayonnaise
½ cup freshly grated Parmesan cheese
¼ teaspoon reduced-sodium Worcestershire
  sauce
¼ teaspoon hot sauce
⅛ teaspoon garlic powder
2 (14-ounce) cans artichoke hearts, drained
  and chopped
Vegetable cooking spray

Combine first 6 ingredients; gently fold in artichokes. Spoon into a 1-quart casserole coated with cooking spray.

Cover and bake at 350° for 20 minutes or until thoroughly heated. Serve with assorted raw vegetables or low-fat crackers. **Yield: 3¼ cups.**

Microwave Directions
  Combine first 6 ingredients; gently fold in artichokes. Spoon into a 1-quart casserole coated with cooking spray.
  Cover with wax paper, and microwave at MEDIUM (50% power) 12 to 14 minutes, stirring twice.

PER TABLESPOON: 15 CALORIES (18% FROM FAT)
FAT 0.3G (SATURATED FAT 0.2G)
PROTEIN 0.8G CARBOHYDRATE 2.4G
CHOLESTEROL 1MG SODIUM 112MG

From left: Baked Wonton Chips (page 16), Sweet Potato Chips, Tortilla Chips (page 16), Pita Chips, and Bagel Chips

Pita Chips

3 (6-inch) whole-wheat pita bread rounds
Butter-flavored vegetable cooking spray
1½ teaspoons lemon juice
1 clove garlic, crushed
1 tablespoon minced fresh parsley
1½ teaspoons minced fresh chives
¼ teaspoon salt
⅛ teaspoon pepper

Separate each pita bread into 2 rounds; cut each into 8 wedges to make 48 triangles. Arrange in a single layer on an ungreased baking sheet, cut side up. Coat with cooking spray.

Combine lemon juice and garlic; lightly brush over each triangle. Combine parsley and remaining ingredients; sprinkle evenly over triangles.

Bake at 350° for 15 minutes or until crisp and lightly browned. Let cool. **Yield: 4 dozen.**

PER CHIP: 11 CALORIES (8% FROM FAT)
FAT 0.1G (SATURATED FAT 0.0G)
PROTEIN 0.2G CARBOHYDRATE 2.0G
CHOLESTEROL 0MG SODIUM 22MG

Bagel Chips

6 plain bagels
Butter-flavored vegetable cooking spray

Cut each bagel horizontally into 6 (¼-inch) slices using an electric slicer or serrated knife. Arrange slices in a single layer on wire racks; place racks on baking sheets. Coat slices with cooking spray.

Bake at 325° for 12 to 15 minutes or until crisp and lightly browned. Remove bagels from oven, and let cool. Store in an airtight container. **Yield: 3 dozen.**

PER CHIP: 26 CALORIES (7% FROM FAT)
FAT 0.2G (SATURATED FAT 0.0G)
PROTEIN 1.0G CARBOHYDRATE 5.1G
CHOLESTEROL 0MG SODIUM 51MG

Variations

Parmesan Cheese Bagel Chips: Sprinkle 2 teaspoons grated Parmesan cheese evenly over bagel chips coated with cooking spray. Bake as directed above. **Yield: 3 dozen.**

PER CHIP: 27 CALORIES (7% FROM FAT)
FAT 0.2G (SATURATED FAT 0.0G)
PROTEIN 1.0G CARBOHYDRATE 5.1G
CHOLESTEROL 0MG SODIUM 52MG

Lemon-and-Herb Bagel Chips: Sprinkle 2 teaspoons salt-free lemon-and-herb spice blend evenly over bagel chips coated with cooking spray. Bake as directed. **Yield: 3 dozen.**

PER CHIP: 27 CALORIES (7% FROM FAT)
FAT 0.2G (SATURATED FAT 0.0G)
PROTEIN 1.0G CARBOHYDRATE 5.3G
CHOLESTEROL 0MG SODIUM 51MG

Garlic Bagel Chips: Sprinkle 1 teaspoon garlic powder evenly over bagel chips coated with cooking spray. Bake as directed. **Yield: 3 dozen.**

PER CHIP: 27 CALORIES (7% FROM FAT)
FAT 0.2G (SATURATED FAT 0.0G)
PROTEIN 1.0G CARBOHYDRATE 5.1G
CHOLESTEROL 0MG SODIUM 51MG

Cinnamon-and-Sugar Bagel Chips: Combine ¼ teaspoon ground cinnamon and 1½ teaspoons sugar; sprinkle mixture evenly over bagel chips coated with cooking spray. Bake as directed. **Yield: 3 dozen.**

PER CHIP: 27 CALORIES (7% FROM FAT)
FAT 0.2G (SATURATED FAT 0.0G)
PROTEIN 1.0G CARBOHYDRATE 5.3G
CHOLESTEROL 0MG SODIUM 51MG

Sweet Potato Chips

1 (½-pound) sweet potato, peeled
Vegetable cooking spray
¼ teaspoon salt

Slice sweet potato crosswise into ⅛-inch slices using a very sharp knife or vegetable cutter. Arrange in a single layer on baking sheets coated with cooking spray. Spray slices with cooking spray.

Bake at 325° for 14 minutes or until crisp. Remove chips from baking sheet as they begin to brown; cool. Sprinkle with salt. Store in an airtight container. **Yield: 3 dozen.**

PER CHIP: 5 CALORIES (18% FROM FAT)
FAT 0.1G (SATURATED FAT 0.0G)
PROTEIN 0.1G CARBOHYDRATE 1.1G
CHOLESTEROL 0MG SODIUM 17MG

Cut the Fat

Nibble your way to better nutrition with crispy Pita Chips and Bagel Chips. Boasting no more than 8% of their calories from fat, they have the crunch of their commercial counterparts but have considerably fewer fat grams and calories.

Tortilla Chips

(pictured on page 14)

12 (6-inch) corn tortillas
½ cup lime juice
¼ cup water
½ teaspoon garlic powder
¼ teaspoon salt
⅛ teaspoon ground cumin
⅛ teaspoon red pepper

Cut 3 (2-inch) rounds from each tortilla using a cookie cutter or kitchen shears. Combine lime juice and water in a small bowl; set aside. Combine garlic powder and remaining ingredients.

Dip tortillas in lime juice mixture; drain on paper towels. Arrange tortillas in a single layer on an ungreased baking sheet; sprinkle evenly with garlic powder mixture.

Bake at 350° for 10 to 12 minutes or until chips are crisp. Cool; store in airtight containers. **Yield: 3 dozen.**

PER CHIP: 6 CALORIES (15% FROM FAT)
FAT 0.1G (SATURATED FAT 0.0G)
PROTEIN 0.2G CARBOHYDRATE 1.4G
CHOLESTEROL 0MG SODIUM 20MG

Baked Wonton Chips

(pictured on page 14)

56 (2-inch-square) wonton skins
Water

Cut wonton skins in half diagonally. Arrange in a single layer on ungreased baking sheets. Spray lightly with water.

Bake at 375° for 8 minutes or until lightly browned. Serve warm or cold. **Yield: 112 chips.**

PER CHIP: 10 CALORIES (9% FROM FAT)
FAT 0.1G (SATURATED FAT 0.0G)
PROTEIN 0.3G CARBOHYDRATE 2.1G
CHOLESTEROL 0MG SODIUM 20MG

Variations

Parmesan Cheese Wonton Chips: Sprinkle 2 teaspoons grated Parmesan cheese evenly over wonton chips sprayed with water. Bake as directed. **Yield: 112 chips.**

PER CHIP: 10 CALORIES (9% FROM FAT)
FAT 0.1G (SATURATED FAT 0.0G)
PROTEIN 0.4G CARBOHYDRATE 2.1G
CHOLESTEROL 0MG SODIUM 21MG

Lemon-and-Herb Wonton Chips: Sprinkle 2 teaspoons salt-free lemon-and-herb spice blend evenly over wonton chips sprayed with water. Bake as directed. **Yield: 112 chips.**

PER CHIP: 11 CALORIES (8% FROM FAT)
FAT 0.1G (SATURATED FAT 0.0G)
PROTEIN 0.4G CARBOHYDRATE 2.1G
CHOLESTEROL 0MG SODIUM 20MG

Garlic Wonton Chips: Sprinkle 1½ teaspoons garlic powder evenly over wonton chips sprayed with water. Bake as directed. **Yield: 112 chips.**

PER CHIP: 10 CALORIES (9% FROM FAT)
FAT 0.1G (SATURATED FAT 0.0G)
PROTEIN 0.4G CARBOHYDRATE 2.1G
CHOLESTEROL 0MG SODIUM 20MG

Cinnamon-and-Sugar Wonton Chips: Combine ¼ teaspoon ground cinnamon and 1½ teaspoons sugar. Sprinkle cinnamon-sugar mixture evenly over wonton chips sprayed with water. Bake as directed. **Yield: 112 chips.**

PER CHIP: 11 CALORIES (8% FROM FAT)
FAT 0.1G (SATURATED FAT 0.0G)
PROTEIN 0.3G CARBOHYDRATE 2.1G
CHOLESTEROL 0MG SODIUM 20MG

From left: Parmesan Pita Chips, Whole Wheat Pretzels (page 18), Snack Mix, and Pita Pizzas (page 18)

Parmesan Pita Chips

4 (6-inch) whole wheat pita bread rounds
⅓ cup commercial oil-free Italian salad
　 dressing
½ cup grated Parmesan cheese
1½ tablespoons sesame seeds

Separate each pita bread into 2 rounds; cut each into 8 wedges to make 64 triangles. Brush inside of each triangle with dressing. Place on ungreased baking sheets, dressing side up.

Combine Parmesan cheese and sesame seeds; sprinkle evenly over triangles.

Bake at 425° for 10 minutes or until lightly browned. Cool on wire racks. Store in an airtight container. **Yield: 64 chips.**

Per Chip: 15 Calories (24% from Fat)
Fat 0.4g (Saturated Fat 0.1g)
Protein 0.5g Carbohydrate 2.2g
Cholesterol 0mg Sodium 48mg

Snack Mix

2 cups toasted oat cereal
2 cups bite-size crispy wheat squares
2 cups bite-size crispy rice squares
2 cups stick pretzels
1½ cups bite-size shredded whole wheat
　 cereal biscuits
Butter-flavored vegetable cooking spray
1½ teaspoons onion powder
1 teaspoon garlic powder
1 teaspoon ground celery seeds
1½ tablespoons reduced-sodium
　 Worcestershire sauce
1 teaspoon hot sauce

Combine first 5 ingredients in a large roasting pan; spray thoroughly with cooking spray.

Combine onion powder and remaining ingredients; distribute over cereal mixture, tossing to coat well.

Bake at 250° for 2 hours, stirring and spraying with cooking spray every 15 minutes. Cool; store in airtight containers. **Yield: 18 (½-cup) servings.**

Per Serving: 74 Calories (10% from Fat)
Fat 0.8g (Saturated Fat 0.2g)
Protein 1.8g Carbohydrate 15.2g
Cholesterol 0mg Sodium 149mg

Snack Smart

Instead of high-fat snacks, try one of these low-fat alternatives; each has less than 5 grams of total fat.

1 apple	2 fig bars
1 bagel	3 gingersnaps
1 banana	1 orange
8 carrot sticks	20 pretzel sticks
½ cup dried fruit	2 rice cakes
1 English muffin	5 vanilla wafers

Pita Pizzas

(pictured on page 17)

1 cup thinly sliced zucchini
¾ cup sliced fresh mushrooms
½ cup sliced green onions
½ cup chopped green pepper
1 cup pizza sauce
8 (6-inch) whole wheat pita bread rounds
Vegetable cooking spray
3 tablespoons grated Parmesan cheese

Combine first 5 ingredients in a medium bowl; toss gently. Place pita rounds on baking sheets coated with cooking spray. Spread ¼ cup zucchini mixture on each pita round; sprinkle evenly with Parmesan cheese.

Bake at 400° for 10 minutes. Cut each round into 8 wedges. Serve hot. Yield: 64 wedges.

PER WEDGE: 25 CALORIES (11% FROM FAT)
FAT 0.3G (SATURATED FAT 0.1G)
PROTEIN 0.6G CARBOHYDRATE 4.5G
CHOLESTEROL 0MG SODIUM 61MG

Potato Skin Snack

2 (6¾-ounce) baking potatoes
Vegetable cooking spray
2 tablespoons commercial oil-free Italian salad dressing
2 teaspoons salt-free herb-and-seasoning blend (regular or spicy)

Scrub potatoes, and coat with cooking spray. Bake at 400° for 1 hour or until done. Allow potatoes to cool.

Cut potatoes in half lengthwise; carefully scoop out pulp, leaving a ¼-inch shell. (Pulp may be reserved for other uses.)

Cut shells into 5 (½-inch-wide) strips. Place strips, skin side down, on a baking sheet. Brush with salad dressing; sprinkle with seasoning blend. Broil 6 inches from heat (with electric oven door partially opened) 5 minutes or until browned. Serve warm. Yield: 20 appetizers.

PER APPETIZER: 7 CALORIES (2% FROM FAT)
FAT 0.0G (SATURATED FAT 0.0G)
PROTEIN 0.2G CARBOHYDRATE 1.6G
CHOLESTEROL 0MG SODIUM 17MG

Whole Wheat Pretzels

(pictured on page 17)

1 package active dry yeast
1 tablespoon sugar
¾ teaspoon salt
1½ cups warm water (105° to 115°)
2¼ cups all-purpose flour
1½ cups whole wheat flour
1 cup (4 ounces) shredded sharp Cheddar cheese
Vegetable cooking spray
1 egg white
2 tablespoons water

Dissolve yeast, sugar, and salt in 1½ cups warm water; let yeast mixture stand 5 minutes.

Combine flours and cheese in a large mixing bowl. Add yeast mixture; beat at low speed of an electric mixer until mixture is well blended. Turn dough out onto a lightly floured surface, and knead until smooth (about 5 minutes).

Cut dough into 32 pieces using kitchen shears dipped in flour; shape each piece into a ball. Roll each ball on a lightly floured surface to form a rope 14 inches long. Twist each into a pretzel shape; place on baking sheets coated with cooking spray.

Combine egg white and 2 tablespoons water; mix well. Brush each pretzel with egg white mixture.

Bake at 425° for 12 to 15 minutes or until lightly browned. Yield: 32 pretzels.

PER PRETZEL: 70 CALORIES (18% FROM FAT)
FAT 1.4G (SATURATED FAT 0.8G)
PROTEIN 2.8G CARBOHYDRATE 11.7G
CHOLESTEROL 4MG SODIUM 79MG

Chicken Wontons
(pictured on page 11)

2 (4-ounce) skinned and boned chicken breast
   halves, cut into ¼-inch strips
1 clove garlic, minced
½ cup shredded carrot
¼ cup finely chopped celery
1 tablespoon low-sodium soy sauce
1 tablespoon dry sherry
1 tablespoon fresh lime juice
2 teaspoons cornstarch
1 teaspoon ground ginger
½ (16-ounce) package wonton wrappers
   (32 wrappers)
Butter-flavored vegetable cooking spray

Position knife blade in food processor bowl;
add chicken. Process 1 minute or until ground.
Cook chicken and garlic in a nonstick skillet over
medium heat, stirring constantly, until chicken is
no longer pink; drain.

Combine chicken, shredded carrot, and next 6
ingredients.

Spoon 1 rounded teaspoon of chicken mixture
into center of each wonton wrapper; moisten
edges with water. Carefully bring 2 opposite
points of wrapper to center over filling; pinch
points together. Bring two remaining opposite
points to center, and pinch together.

Place filled wontons on a baking sheet coated
with cooking spray. Lightly coat each wonton
with cooking spray.

Bake at 375° for 8 to 10 minutes or until lightly browned. **Yield: 32 wontons.**

PER WONTON: 33 CALORIES (11% FROM FAT)
FAT 0.4G (SATURATED FAT 0.1G)
PROTEIN 2.3G CARBOHYDRATE 4.6G
CHOLESTEROL 5MG SODIUM 58MG

Tortellini with Rosemary-Parmesan Sauce
(pictured on page 11)

2½ tablespoons nonfat dry milk
⅔ cup skim milk
1⅔ cups nonfat cottage cheese
¼ cup grated Parmesan cheese
¼ cup chopped fresh chives
1 tablespoon lemon juice
1¾ teaspoons chopped fresh rosemary
¼ teaspoon pepper
¼ teaspoon salt
1 (9-ounce) package refrigerated cheese-filled
   tortellini, cooked without salt or fat
1 (9-ounce) package refrigerated cheese-filled
   spinach tortellini, cooked without salt
   or fat
Garnish: fresh chives

Position knife blade in food processor bowl;
add dry milk and skim milk. Process 10 seconds
or until blended.

Add cottage cheese and next 6 ingredients;
process 1 minute, stopping once to scrape down
sides of bowl.

Cover and chill thoroughly. Serve sauce with
tortellini and garnish, if desired. **Yield: 20 servings.**

PER SERVING: 92 CALORIES (23% FROM FAT)
FAT 2.4G (SATURATED FAT 0.7G)
PROTEIN 7.3G CARBOHYDRATE 10.4G
CHOLESTEROL 16MG SODIUM 209MG

Special-Occasion Appetizer

Pair cheese-filled tortellini with
Rosemary-Parmesan Sauce. Refrigerated tortellini can be stored in
the refrigerator up to 5 days or
frozen up to 4 months. Cooking
time is less than 10 minutes.

Clockwise from top: Spiced Pineapple Sparkle, Mock Black Russian, Mock Eggnog with Orange and Nutmeg, and Spicy Virgin Mary (page 22)

Spiced Pineapple Sparkle

1½ cups water
6 (3-inch) sticks cinnamon
12 whole cloves
½ cup sugar
1 (46-ounce) can unsweetened pineapple juice, chilled
1½ cups unsweetened orange juice, chilled
½ cup lemon juice, chilled
3 (12-ounce) bottles lemon-lime carbonated beverage, chilled
Garnishes: orange slices, maraschino cherries

Combine first 3 ingredients in a saucepan; bring to a boil. Cover, reduce heat, and simmer 15 minutes. Remove from heat, and stir in sugar; let cool.

Pour mixture through a large, wire-mesh strainer into a punch bowl, discarding spices; stir in juices and lemon-lime beverage. Garnish, if desired. **Yield: 12 (1-cup) servings.**

PER SERVING: 147 CALORIES (1% FROM FAT)
FAT 0.1G (SATURATED FAT 0.0G)
PROTEIN 0.6G CARBOHYDRATE 37.0G
CHOLESTEROL 0MG SODIUM 2MG

Mock Black Russian

1½ tablespoons instant coffee granules
1 cup boiling water
1 quart low-fat vanilla ice cream, divided
½ cup chocolate syrup, divided
2 teaspoons vanilla extract
2 teaspoons semisweet chocolate shavings

Dissolve coffee granules in boiling water; let coffee cool.

Place half of ice cream and half of chocolate syrup in container of an electric blender; cover and process until smooth, stopping to scrape down sides. Pour into a large bowl or pitcher.

Repeat with remaining ice cream and syrup, and add to bowl. Add coffee and vanilla; stir with a wire whisk.

Pour into glasses; sprinkle each with ¼ teaspoon chocolate shavings. Serve immediately. **Yield: 8 (5-ounce) servings.**

PER SERVING: 150 CALORIES (20% FROM FAT)
FAT 3.4G (SATURATED FAT 1.9G)
PROTEIN 3.3G CARBOHYDRATE 27.1G
CHOLESTEROL 9MG SODIUM 69MG

Mock Eggnog with Orange and Nutmeg

2 tablespoons sugar
2 tablespoons cornstarch
1 quart skim milk
1 teaspoon vanilla extract
½ teaspoon rum extract
½ teaspoon grated orange rind
⅛ teaspoon salt
⅓ cup sugar, divided
1 tablespoon meringue powder
½ cup cold water
Ground nutmeg (optional)

Combine sugar and cornstarch in a medium saucepan; stir in milk. Bring to a boil over medium heat, stirring constantly. Boil mixture, stirring constantly, 1 minute. Remove from heat.

Stir in vanilla and next 3 ingredients; cover and chill.

Combine 3 tablespoons sugar, meringue powder, and water in a large mixing bowl just before serving. Beat at high speed of an electric mixer 5 minutes; gradually add remaining 2⅓ tablespoons sugar, beating until soft peaks form.

Fold into milk mixture. Sprinkle with nutmeg, if desired. **Yield: 7 (¾-cup) servings.**

PER SERVING: 115 CALORIES (2% FROM FAT)
FAT 0.2G (SATURATED FAT 0.2G)
PROTEIN 5.6G CARBOHYDRATE 22.1G
CHOLESTEROL 3MG SODIUM 127MG

Spicy Virgin Mary

(pictured on page 20)

1 (48-ounce) can low-sodium tomato juice
1 (13¾-ounce) can ready-to-serve, no-salt-added beef broth
¼ cup low-sodium Worcestershire sauce
3 tablespoons lime juice
1½ teaspoons seasoned salt
1 teaspoon celery seeds
½ teaspoon onion powder
½ teaspoon freshly ground pepper
⅛ teaspoon garlic powder
¼ teaspoon hot sauce
Ice cubes
Garnish: celery stalks

Combine first 10 ingredients; chill. Serve over ice and garnish, if desired. **Yield: 8 (1-cup) servings.**

PER SERVING: 49 CALORIES (2% FROM FAT)
FAT 0.1G (SATURATED FAT 0.0G)
PROTEIN 1.9G CARBOHYDRATE 11.4G
CHOLESTEROL 0MG SODIUM 437MG

White Grape Punch

1 (48-ounce) bottle apple juice
1 (24-ounce) bottle white grape juice
1 (12-ounce) can frozen lemonade concentrate, thawed and undiluted
1 (33.8-ounce) bottle club soda, chilled

Combine first 3 ingredients; chill well. Stir in club soda just before serving. **Yield: 14 (1-cup) servings.**

PER SERVING: 127 CALORIES (1% FROM FAT)
FAT 0.2G (SATURATED FAT 0.0G)
PROTEIN 0.1G CARBOHYDRATE 32.4G
CHOLESTEROL 0MG SODIUM 21MG

Bourbon Blizzard

½ gallon low-fat vanilla ice cream, divided
½ gallon 1% low-fat milk, divided
¾ cup bourbon
¼ cup vanilla extract
1 tablespoon ground nutmeg
Additional ground nutmeg

Combine 2 cups ice cream, 2 cups milk, bourbon, vanilla, and 1 tablespoon nutmeg in container of an electric blender; cover and process until smooth. Pour into a large bowl.

Add one-third each of remaining ice cream and milk to blender; cover and process until smooth, stopping once to scrape down sides. Add to bowl. Repeat procedure twice with remaining ice cream and milk. Stir with a wire whisk. Cover; chill.

Pour into punch cups, and sprinkle with additional nutmeg. **Yield: 26 (½-cup) servings.**

PER SERVING: 138 CALORIES (23% FROM FAT)
FAT 3.5G (SATURATED FAT 2.2G)
PROTEIN 4.7G CARBOHYDRATE 17.7G
CHOLESTEROL 11MG SODIUM 89MG

Sugar-Free Spiced Tea Mix

1 (3.3-ounce) jar sugar-free, caffeine-free iced tea mix with lemon
2 (1.8-ounce) packages sugar-free orange breakfast drink mix
1 tablespoon plus 1 teaspoon ground cinnamon
2 teaspoons ground cloves

Combine all ingredients, and store in an airtight container. To serve, stir 1½ teaspoons mix into 1 cup hot water. **Yield: 96 (1-cup) servings.**

PER SERVING: 6 CALORIES (3% FROM FAT)
FAT 0.0G (SATURATED FAT 0.0G)
PROTEIN 0.1G CARBOHYDRATE 1.1G
CHOLESTEROL 0MG SODIUM 6MG

Breads

Freshly baked biscuits, cornbread, and yeast breads can remain dinnertime staples. It will be hard to tell the difference between these lightened-up recipes and their original counterparts.

Whole Wheat Biscuits, Granola Muffins, Oatmeal-Bran Muffins

Old-Fashioned Cinnamon Rolls, Herbed Bread, English Muffin Bread, Spoonbread

Fruity Banana Bread, Cinnamon-Oat Bread, Honey Pancakes, Cornmeal Muffins

Jalapeño Cornbread, Yogurt Crescent Rolls, Parsley-Garlic Rolls

Mini Swiss Cheese Loaves (page 32)

Whole Wheat Biscuits

Whole Wheat Biscuits

1½ cups all-purpose flour
½ cup whole wheat flour
1 tablespoon baking powder
½ teaspoon salt
3 tablespoons reduced-calorie margarine
¾ cup evaporated skimmed milk
Vegetable cooking spray

Combine flours, baking powder, and salt; cut in margarine with a pastry blender until mixture is crumbly.

Add milk, stirring until dry ingredients are moistened. Turn dough out onto a lightly floured surface, and knead about 1 minute.

Shape dough into 12 balls; place balls in an 8-inch square pan coated with cooking spray.

Flatten dough slightly. Bake at 450° for 10 to 12 minutes or until golden. **Yield: 1 dozen.**

PER BISCUIT: 105 CALORIES (19% FROM FAT)
FAT 2.2G (SATURATED FAT 0.3G)
PROTEIN 3.6G CARBOHYDRATE 18.2G
CHOLESTEROL 1MG SODIUM 144MG

Granola Muffins

1½ cups reduced-fat biscuit mix
1 cup firmly packed brown sugar
1 teaspoon ground cinnamon
1 cup oats and honey granola cereal with
   almonds
½ cup raisins
1 large egg, lightly beaten
¾ cup skim milk
1 tablespoon vegetable oil
Vegetable cooking spray

Combine first 3 ingredients in a bowl; stir in cereal and raisins. Make a well in center; set flour mixture aside.

Combine egg, milk, and oil; add to flour mixture, stirring just until dry ingredients are moistened. (Batter will be thin.)

Coat muffin cups with cooking spray; spoon batter into cups, filling three-fourths full.

Bake at 375° for 15 to 20 minutes or until golden. **Yield: 16 muffins.**

PER MUFFIN: 140 CALORIES (21% FROM FAT)
FAT 3.3G (SATURATED FAT 0.7G)
PROTEIN 2.5G CARBOHYDRATE 25.1G
CHOLESTEROL 14MG SODIUM 153MG

Oatmeal-Bran Muffins

¾ cup morsels of wheat bran cereal
¾ cup regular oats, uncooked
1¼ cups skim milk
1 egg or ¼ cup egg substitute
¼ cup vegetable oil
½ cup raisins
1¼ cups all-purpose flour
1 tablespoon baking powder
½ teaspoon salt
½ cup sugar
Vegetable cooking spray

Combine first 3 ingredients in a bowl; let stand 5 minutes. Stir in egg, oil, and raisins.

Combine flour, baking powder, salt, and sugar; make a well in center of mixture. Add bran mixture, stirring just until moistened.

Spoon batter into muffin pans coated with cooking spray, filling three-fourths full. Bake at 400° for 20 to 25 minutes. **Yield: 1½ dozen.**

PER MUFFIN: 127 CALORIES (28% FROM FAT)
FAT 4.0G (SATURATED FAT 0.7G)
PROTEIN 3.0G CARBOHYDRATE 21.4G
CHOLESTEROL 13MG SODIUM 100MG

Apricot-Orange Bread

(pictured on page 11)

1 (6-ounce) package dried apricots, diced
¾ cup firmly packed brown sugar
1 cup nonfat buttermilk
½ cup egg substitute
3 tablespoons vegetable oil
1 tablespoon grated orange rind
1¼ teaspoons vanilla extract
¼ teaspoon almond extract
1½ cups all-purpose flour
¾ cup whole wheat flour
1½ teaspoons baking powder
1 teaspoon baking soda
½ teaspoon salt
Vegetable cooking spray
Garnishes: dried apricots, orange rind strips, cinnamon sticks, grape leaves

Combine first 8 ingredients; let stand 5 minutes. Combine all-purpose flour and next 4 ingredients in a large bowl; make a well in center of mixture. Add apricot mixture to dry ingredients, stirring just until moistened.

Coat either a 6-cup Bundt pan or 9- x 5- x 3-inch loafpan with cooking spray. Spoon batter into pan.

Bake at 350° for 35 minutes or until a wooden pick inserted in center comes out clean. Cool in pan on a wire rack 10 minutes; remove from pan, and cool on wire rack. Garnish, if desired. **Yield: 21 slices.**

PER SLICE: 111 CALORIES (19% FROM FAT)
FAT 2.3G (SATURATED FAT 0.4G)
PROTEIN 2.8G CARBOHYDRATE 20.6G
CHOLESTEROL 0MG SODIUM 145MG

Fruity Banana Bread

Vegetable cooking spray
⅓ cup margarine, softened
¾ cup sugar
½ cup egg substitute
1¾ cups all-purpose flour
2¾ teaspoons baking powder
1 cup mashed banana
¾ cup coarsely chopped mixed dried fruit

Coat an 8½- x 4½- x 3-inch loafpan with cooking spray; set aside.

Beat margarine at medium speed of an electric mixer until creamy; gradually add ¾ cup sugar, beating well. Add egg substitute, beating until blended.

Combine all-purpose flour and baking powder; add to margarine mixture. Beat at low speed until blended. Stir in mashed banana and dried fruit. Pour batter into prepared loafpan.

Bake at 350° for 1 hour or until a wooden pick inserted in center of loaf comes out clean. Cool in pan on a wire rack 10 minutes; remove from pan, and cool completely on wire rack. **Yield: 16 (½-inch) slices.**

PER SLICE: 149 CALORIES (23% FROM FAT)
FAT 3.8G (SATURATED FAT 0.7G)
PROTEIN 2.3G CARBOHYDRATE 27.3G
CHOLESTEROL 0MG SODIUM 54MG

Waffles

1¾ cups all-purpose flour
1¼ teaspoons baking powder
2 tablespoons sugar
1 large egg, separated
1 cup skim milk
2 tablespoons plus 2 teaspoons reduced-calorie stick margarine, melted
1 egg white
Vegetable cooking spray

Combine first 3 ingredients in a medium bowl; make a well in center of mixture.

Beat egg yolk in a small bowl; add milk and margarine, stirring well. Add liquid mixture to dry ingredients, stirring until smooth.

Beat 2 egg whites at high speed of an electric mixer until stiff peaks form; fold beaten egg whites into batter.

Coat waffle iron with cooking spray; allow waffle iron to preheat. For each waffle, pour ½ cup batter onto hot waffle iron, spreading batter to edges. Bake 4 to 5 minutes or until steaming stops. Repeat procedure with remaining batter. **Yield: 20 (3-inch) waffles.**

PER WAFFLE: 63 CALORIES (21% FROM FAT)
FAT 1.5G (SATURATED FAT 0.2G)
PROTEIN 2.0G CARBOHYDRATE 10.3G
CHOLESTEROL 11MG SODIUM 27MG

Honey Pancakes

3 cups all-purpose flour
2 tablespoons baking powder
½ teaspoon salt
3 cups skim milk
½ cup egg substitute
¼ cup honey
¼ cup vegetable oil
Vegetable cooking spray

Combine first 3 ingredients in a large bowl. Combine milk and next 3 ingredients; add to flour mixture, stirring until smooth.

Pour about ¼ cup batter for each pancake onto a hot griddle coated with cooking spray. Turn pancakes when tops are covered with bubbles and edges look cooked. **Yield: 28 (4-inch) pancakes.**

PER PANCAKE: 88 CALORIES (23% FROM FAT)
FAT 2.2G (SATURATED FAT 0.4G)
PROTEIN 2.7G CARBOHYDRATE 14.3G
CHOLESTEROL 1MG SODIUM 62MG

Honey Pancakes

Cornmeal Muffins

Cornmeal Muffins

1 cup yellow cornmeal
1 cup all-purpose flour
2 teaspoons baking powder
1 teaspoon baking soda
½ teaspoon salt
1 teaspoon sugar
¼ cup egg substitute or 2 egg whites
1¼ cups plain nonfat yogurt
2½ tablespoons vegetable oil
Vegetable cooking spray

Combine first 6 ingredients in a large bowl; make a well in center of mixture. Combine egg substitute, yogurt, and oil; add to dry ingredients, stirring just until moistened.

Spoon mixture into muffin pans coated with cooking spray, filling three-fourths full.

Bake at 425° for 12 to 14 minutes or until golden. Remove muffins from pans immediately. **Yield: 1½ dozen.**

PER MUFFIN: 80 CALORIES (28% FROM FAT)
FAT 2.5G (SATURATED FAT 0.4G)
PROTEIN 2.5G CARBOHYDRATE 12.1G
CHOLESTEROL 0MG SODIUM 155MG

Jalapeño Cornbread

1 cup cornmeal
2 teaspoons baking powder
¼ teaspoon salt
2 large eggs
3 tablespoons nonfat sour cream
1½ teaspoons vegetable oil
1 (8¾-ounce) can cream-style corn
1 (4.25-ounce) jar pickled, chopped jalapeño
     peppers, drained
Vegetable cooking spray

Heat an 8-inch cast-iron skillet in a 400° oven for 5 minutes.

Combine first 3 ingredients in a large bowl; make a well in center of mixture. Set aside.

Combine eggs and next 4 ingredients; add to dry ingredients, stirring until moistened.

Remove skillet from oven, and coat with cooking spray; pour batter into hot skillet.

Bake at 400° for 20 minutes or until golden. **Yield: 8 servings.**

Note: For best results use whole eggs, not egg substitute.

PER SERVING: 178 CALORIES (21% FROM FAT)
FAT 4.1G (SATURATED FAT 0.8G)
PROTEIN 6.8G CARBOHYDRATE 28.4G
CHOLESTEROL 74MG SODIUM 684MG

Spoonbread

1 cup white cornmeal
2 cups evaporated skimmed milk
1 cup water
2 tablespoons reduced-calorie margarine
½ teaspoon salt
2 egg whites
½ cup egg substitute
Vegetable cooking spray

Combine first 5 ingredients; cook mixture over medium heat, stirring constantly, 5 minutes or until thickened. Remove from heat.

Beat egg whites at medium speed of an electric mixer until stiff. With mixer running, slowly add egg substitute. Gradually stir about one-third of hot mixture into egg mixture; add to remaining hot mixture, stirring constantly. Pour into a 1½-quart casserole coated with cooking spray.

Bake at 350° for 35 minutes or until a knife inserted in center comes out clean. **Yield: 9 (½-cup) servings.**

PER SERVING: 118 CALORIES (18% FROM FAT)
FAT 2.3G (SATURATED FAT 0.4G)
PROTEIN 7.5G CARBOHYDRATE 17.2G
CHOLESTEROL 2MG SODIUM 256MG

Old-Fashioned Cinnamon Rolls

Old-Fashioned Cinnamon Rolls

⅓ cup skim milk
⅓ cup reduced-calorie margarine
¼ cup firmly packed brown sugar
1 teaspoon salt
1 package active dry yeast
½ cup warm water (105° to 115°)
½ cup egg substitute
3½ cups bread flour, divided
¾ cup quick-cooking oats, uncooked
Vegetable cooking spray
¼ cup reduced-calorie margarine, softened
¾ cup firmly packed brown sugar
¼ cup raisins
2 teaspoons ground cinnamon
1 cup sifted powdered sugar
2 tablespoons water

Combine first 4 ingredients in a saucepan; heat until margarine melts, stirring occasionally. Cool mixture to 105° to 115°.

Combine yeast and warm water; let stand 5 minutes. Combine yeast mixture, milk mixture, egg substitute, 1 cup flour, and oats in a large mixing bowl, mixing well. Gradually stir in enough remaining flour to make a soft dough.

Turn dough out onto a lightly floured surface; knead until smooth and elastic (about 8 minutes). Place dough in a large bowl coated with cooking spray, turning to grease top.

Cover and let rise in a warm place (85°), free from drafts, 1 hour or until doubled in bulk.

Punch dough down. Cover; let rest 10 minutes. Divide in half; roll each half into a 12-inch square. Spread each with 2 tablespoons margarine.

Combine ¾ cup brown sugar, raisins, and cinnamon; sprinkle over each square. Roll up jelly-roll fashion; pinch seam to seal. Cut each roll into 1-inch slices; place, cut side down, in two 8-inch square pans coated with cooking spray.

Cover; let rise in a warm place, free from drafts, 30 minutes or until almost doubled in bulk.

Bake at 375° for 15 to 20 minutes or until golden. Combine powdered sugar and 2 tablespoons water; drizzle over warm rolls. **Yield: 2 dozen.**

Per Roll: 159 Calories (19% from Fat)
Fat 3.4g (Saturated Fat 0.5g)
Protein 3.6g Carbohydrate 29.0g
Cholesterol 0mg Sodium 153mg

Yogurt Crescent Rolls

⅓ cup vegetable oil
1 (8-ounce) carton plain low-fat yogurt
½ cup sugar
2 packages active dry yeast
½ cup warm water (105° to 115°)
1 large egg
1 egg white
4 cups all-purpose flour
1 teaspoon salt
Butter-flavored vegetable cooking spray

Combine first 3 ingredients in a large bowl.

Combine yeast and warm water; let stand 5 minutes. Stir yeast, egg, and egg white into yogurt.

Combine flour and salt. Stir 2 cups flour mixture into yogurt mixture; beat at medium speed of an electric mixer until smooth. Gradually stir in remaining flour mixture. Cover and chill 8 hours.

Punch dough down, and divide into 4 equal portions. Roll each portion to a 10-inch circle on a floured surface; coat with cooking spray. Cut each circle into 12 wedges; roll up each wedge, beginning at wide end. Place on baking sheets coated with cooking spray, point side down.

Cover and let rise in a warm place (85°), free from drafts, 45 minutes or until doubled in bulk.

Bake at 375° for 10 to 12 minutes or until rolls are golden. **Yield: 4 dozen.**

Per Roll: 66 Calories (25% from Fat)
Fat 1.8g (Saturated Fat 0.4g)
Protein 1.7g Carbohydrate 10.6g
Cholesterol 5mg Sodium 55mg

Parsley-Garlic Rolls

2 tablespoons reduced-calorie margarine, melted
2 cloves garlic, crushed
1 (16-ounce) loaf frozen bread dough, thawed
1 tablespoon chopped fresh parsley
Vegetable cooking spray

Combine margarine and garlic; set aside.

Cut bread dough crosswise into 6 even portions with kitchen shears; cut portions in half crosswise. Roll each half to ¼-inch thickness on a lightly floured surface; brush with margarine mixture, and sprinkle with parsley. Roll each piece of dough, jellyroll fashion, and place, swirled side down, in muffin pans coated with cooking spray.

Cover and let rise in a warm place (85°), free from drafts, 1 hour or until doubled in bulk. Bake at 400° for 10 to 12 minutes. Serve immediately. **Yield: 1 dozen.**

PER ROLL: 97 CALORIES (20% FROM FAT)
FAT 2.2G (SATURATED FAT 0.2G)
PROTEIN 3.0G CARBOHYDRATE 16.1G
CHOLESTEROL 0MG SODIUM 196MG

Mini Swiss Cheese Loaves

(pictured on page 23)

1 package active dry yeast
¼ cup warm water (105° to 115°)
2⅓ cups all-purpose flour, divided
1 teaspoon salt
¼ teaspoon baking soda
2 tablespoons sugar
1 (8-ounce) carton plain nonfat yogurt
1 large egg
1 cup (4 ounces) shredded reduced-fat Swiss cheese
Vegetable cooking spray
2 teaspoons sesame seeds, toasted

Combine yeast and warm water in a 1-cup liquid measuring cup; let stand 5 minutes.

Combine yeast mixture, 1 cup flour, and next 5 ingredients in a large mixing bowl.

Beat at low speed of an electric mixer 30 seconds. Beat at high speed 2 minutes, scraping bowl occasionally.

Stir in remaining 1⅓ cups flour and cheese, mixing well.

Divide batter evenly among 8 (5- x 3- x 2-inch) loafpans coated with cooking spray; sprinkle evenly with sesame seeds.

Cover and let rise in a warm place (85°), free from drafts, 1 hour. (Batter may not double in bulk.)

Bake at 350° for 25 minutes or until golden. Remove from pans; serve warm, or cool on wire racks. **Yield: 16 (½-loaf) servings.**

Note: For reduced-fat Swiss cheese, we used Alpine Lace.

PER SERVING: 113 CALORIES (20% FROM FAT)
FAT 2.5G (SATURATED FAT 1.1G)
PROTEIN 5.3G CARBOHYDRATE 17.1G
CHOLESTEROL 19MG SODIUM 190MG

Cinnamon-Oat Bread

1⅔ cups bread flour
1 cup regular oats, uncooked
½ cup unprocessed oat bran
1½ teaspoons salt
3 packages active dry yeast
1¾ cups water
½ cup honey
½ cup vegetable oil
½ cup egg substitute
2½ cups whole wheat flour
1¾ cups bread flour, divided
Butter-flavored vegetable cooking spray
1 tablespoon sugar
2 teaspoons ground cinnamon

Cinnamon-Oat Bread

Combine first 5 ingredients in a large mixing bowl. Combine water, honey, and oil in a medium saucepan; heat to 120° to 130°.

Add liquid mixture and egg substitute gradually to flour mixture; beat at low speed of an electric mixer until blended. Beat 3 additional minutes at medium speed. Gradually stir in wheat flour and ¼ cup bread flour to form a soft dough.

Turn dough out onto a lightly floured surface. Knead until smooth and elastic (about 10 minutes); add enough of remaining 1½ cups bread flour to prevent dough from sticking to hands.

Place dough in a large bowl coated with cooking spray, turning to coat top. Cover and let rise in a warm place (85°), free from drafts, 1 hour or until doubled in bulk.

Punch dough down; let rest 15 minutes. Divide in half. Roll each portion to a 15- x 7-inch

rectangle on a lightly floured surface. Coat dough with butter-flavored cooking spray. Combine sugar and cinnamon; sprinkle over dough.

Roll up dough, jellyroll fashion, starting with narrow end. Place, seam side down, in 2 (9- x 5- x 3-inch) loafpans coated with cooking spray. Let dough rise in a warm place, free from drafts, 30 minutes or until loaves are doubled in bulk.

Bake at 375° for 35 minutes or until loaves sound hollow when tapped. (Cover loaves loosely with aluminum foil for the last 20 minutes of baking to prevent overbrowning, if necessary.) Remove from pans immediately; cool. **Yield: 2 loaves or 36 (½-inch) slices.**

PER SERVING: 137 CALORIES (24% FROM FAT)
FAT 3.7G (SATURATED FAT 0.6G)
PROTEIN 3.9G CARBOHYDRATE 22.8G
CHOLESTEROL 0MG SODIUM 104MG

Herbed Bread

¼ cup margarine
1¼ cups water
2 cups whole wheat flour
1 package active dry yeast
1 teaspoon onion powder
¼ teaspoon salt
¼ teaspoon white pepper
2 tablespoons instant nonfat dry milk powder
2 tablespoons honey
1¾ cups all-purpose flour, divided
Vegetable cooking spray
1 tablespoon margarine, melted
¼ cup minced fresh parsley
1 tablespoon minced fresh thyme
¾ teaspoon minced fresh sage
¾ teaspoon minced fresh rosemary

Combine ¼ cup margarine and water in a saucepan; heat to 120° to 130°. Set aside.

Combine whole wheat flour and next 6 ingredients in a large mixing bowl; add margarine mixture. Beat at medium speed of an electric mixer until smooth. Stir in 1½ cups all-purpose flour. Turn dough out onto a lightly floured surface. Knead dough 5 minutes, using remaining ¼ cup flour.

Place dough in a bowl coated with cooking spray, turning dough to coat top. Cover and let rise in a warm place (85°), free from drafts, 1 hour or until doubled in bulk.

Punch dough down; turn out onto a lightly floured surface. Roll into a 15- x 9-inch rectangle; brush with melted margarine.

Combine parsley and remaining herbs; stir well. Sprinkle over dough. Roll up, jellyroll fashion, starting with narrow end. Place, seam side down, in a 9- x 5- x 3-inch loafpan coated with cooking spray. Let rise in a warm place (85°), free from drafts, 45 minutes or until doubled in bulk.

Bake at 350° for 45 minutes or until golden.

Remove loaf from pan, and cool slightly on a wire rack. **Yield: 18 (½-inch) slices.**

PER SLICE: 134 CALORIES (24% FROM FAT)
FAT 3.6G (SATURATED FAT 0.7G)
PROTEIN 3.7G CARBOHYDRATE 22.4G
CHOLESTEROL 0MG SODIUM 76MG

English Muffin Bread

3½ to 3¾ cups all-purpose flour, divided
1 cup whole wheat flour
½ cup oat bran
2 teaspoons salt
1 package rapid-rise yeast
1 cup skim milk
1 cup water
3 tablespoons reduced-calorie margarine
Vegetable cooking spray
2 tablespoons cornmeal

Combine 1½ cups all-purpose flour and next 4 ingredients in a large bowl; set aside.

Combine skim milk, water, and margarine in a 4-cup liquid measuring cup. Microwave at HIGH 2 minutes; pour over flour mixture.

Beat mixture at medium speed of an electric mixer 2 minutes. Stir in 2 cups all-purpose flour. Turn dough out onto a lightly floured surface; if dough is sticky, knead in remaining ¼ cup flour. Cover with a large bowl; let stand 10 minutes.

Coat 2 (8½- x 4½- x 3-inch) loafpans with cooking spray; sprinkle evenly with cornmeal. Divide dough in half; shape each portion into a loaf, and place in pan.

Cover; let rise in a warm place (85°), free from drafts, 1 hour or until doubled in bulk.

Bake at 400° for 25 minutes. Remove loaves from pans, and cool on wire racks. **Yield: 2 loaves or 32 (½-inch) slices.**

PER SLICE: 77 CALORIES (10% FROM FAT)
FAT 0.9G (SATURATED FAT 0.1G)
PROTEIN 2.5G CARBOHYDRATE 14.6G
CHOLESTEROL 0MG SODIUM 154MG

Desserts

These dazzling light desserts will please the eye as well as the palate. Each one conquers the myth that dessert must be high in calories, fat, and sugar to be delicious.

Angel Food Trifle, Peach Sherbet, Raspberry-Cherry Cobbler

Oatmeal-Raisin Cookies, Chocolate-Hazelnut Biscotti, Flaky Apple Turnovers

Banana-Coconut Cake, Frosted Carrot Cake, Strawberry Shortcake, Buttermilk Pie

Old-Fashioned Banana Pudding, Orange-Coconut Angel Food Cake

Pound Cake (page 39), Buttermilk Pie (page 46), and Fresh Strawberry Ice Milk (page 50)

Orange-Coconut Angel Food Cake

1 (16-ounce) package angel food cake mix
1 cup water
⅓ cup freshly squeezed orange juice
2 teaspoons orange extract, divided
1 (3-ounce) package vanilla pudding mix
2 cups skim milk
1 tablespoon grated orange rind
2 cups flaked coconut, divided
2½ cups reduced-fat frozen whipped topping, thawed and divided

Prepare cake mix according to package directions, using 1 cup water and ⅓ cup orange juice instead of liquid called for on package. Stir in 1 teaspoon orange extract. Spoon evenly into an ungreased 10-inch tube pan.

Bake at 375° on lowest oven rack for 30 minutes or until cake springs back when lightly touched. Invert pan; cool completely. Loosen cake from sides of pan, using a narrow metal spatula; remove from pan, and slice horizontally into 4 equal layers; set aside.

Combine pudding mix and skim milk in a large saucepan; bring to a boil over medium heat, stirring constantly. Remove from heat, and stir in remaining 1 teaspoon orange extract and orange rind. Cool mixture. Fold in 1 cup coconut and 1 cup whipped topping.

Place bottom cake layer on a serving plate; spread top of layer with one-third of pudding mixture. Repeat procedure with remaining cake layers and pudding mixture, ending with top cake layer.

Spread remaining 1½ cups whipped topping on top and sides of cake; sprinkle with remaining 1 cup coconut. Store in refrigerator. **Yield: 16 servings.**

PER SERVING: 193 CALORIES (21% FROM FAT)
FAT 4.5G (SATURATED FAT 2.5G)
PROTEIN 4.0G CARBOHYDRATE 33.8G
CHOLESTEROL 1MG SODIUM 301MG

Angel Food Trifle

1 (16-ounce) package angel food cake mix
⅓ cup sugar
¼ cup cornstarch
¼ teaspoon salt
2 cups skim milk
¼ cup egg substitute
1 teaspoon grated lemon rind
¼ cup lemon juice
2 (8-ounce) cartons vanilla low-fat yogurt
2 cups sliced strawberries
3 kiwifruit, sliced
3 strawberry fans

Prepare cake mix according to package directions. Cut into bite-size cubes; set aside.

Combine sugar, cornstarch, and salt in a saucepan; gradually add milk, stirring well. Cook over medium heat until mixture begins to thicken, stirring constantly.

Remove mixture from heat; gradually add egg substitute, stirring constantly with a wire whisk. Cook over medium-low heat 2 minutes, stirring constantly.

Remove from heat; cool slightly. Stir in lemon rind and lemon juice; chill. Fold yogurt into custard mixture; set aside.

Place one-third of cake in bottom of a 16-cup trifle bowl. Spoon one-third of custard over cake; arrange half each of strawberry slices and kiwi slices around lower edge of bowl and over custard. Repeat process with remaining ingredients, ending with strawberry fans on top.

Cover and chill 3 to 4 hours. **Yield: 15 (⅔-cup) servings.**

PER SERVING: 193 CALORIES (3% FROM FAT)
FAT 0.7G (SATURATED FAT 0.3G)
PROTEIN 6.0G CARBOHYDRATE 41.5G
CHOLESTEROL 2MG SODIUM 305MG

Angel Food Trifle

Lemon Angel Rolls

Lemon Angel Rolls

1 angel food cake loaf
¼ cup Key Largo liqueur
1 (11¼-ounce) jar lemon curd
Sifted powdered sugar
Raspberry Sauce
Garnishes: lemon twist, fresh mint sprigs

Remove crust from cake. Cut cake horizontally into 8 slices; flatten each slice slightly with a rolling pin. Brush with liqueur. Spread each cake slice with 1½ tablespoons lemon curd. Starting from the narrow end, roll up cake jellyroll fashion.

Wrap filled cake rolls in wax paper; chill. Cut each into thirds; sprinkle with sugar.

Spoon 1½ tablespoons Raspberry Sauce onto each dessert plate; arrange 3 cake roll slices on sauce. Garnish, if desired. **Yield: 8 servings.**

Raspberry Sauce

1 (10-ounce) package frozen raspberries in
    light syrup, thawed
2 teaspoons cornstarch

Place raspberries in container of an electric blender; process until smooth. Pour mixture through a wire-mesh strainer into a small saucepan. Stir in cornstarch; place over medium heat, stirring constantly, until mixture thickens and boils. Boil 1 minute, stirring constantly. Remove from heat, and let cool. **Yield: ¾ cup.**

PER SERVING: 331 CALORIES (19% FROM FAT)
FAT 6.9G (SATURATED FAT 1.5G)
PROTEIN 4.3G CARBOHYDRATE 60.7G
CHOLESTEROL 65MG SODIUM 168MG

Banana-Coconut Cake

1¾ cups all-purpose flour
½ teaspoon baking soda
¼ teaspoon salt
⅓ cup sugar
1¼ teaspoons cream of tartar
¾ cup mashed ripe banana
¼ cup egg substitute
¼ cup skim milk
¼ cup margarine, melted
1 teaspoon vanilla extract
1 tablespoon flaked coconut
¼ teaspoon ground cinnamon
Vegetable cooking spray

Combine first 5 ingredients in a large bowl; make a well in center of mixture. Combine banana and next 4 ingredients; add to dry mixture, stirring until moistened. Combine coconut and cinnamon; set aside.

Coat an 8-inch square pan with cooking spray. Spoon batter into pan; sprinkle with coconut mixture.

Bake at 350° for 20 to 25 minutes or until a wooden pick inserted in center comes out clean. Cool in pan on a wire rack 5 minutes. Remove from pan; let cool on wire rack. **Yield: 8 servings.**

PER SERVING: 230 CALORIES (25% FROM FAT)
FAT 6.5G (SATURATED FAT 1.5G)
PROTEIN 4.3G CARBOHYDRATE 39.3G
CHOLESTEROL 0MG SODIUM 241MG

Frosted Carrot Cake

1½ cups all-purpose flour
⅔ cup whole wheat flour
2 teaspoons baking soda
2 teaspoons ground cinnamon
¼ teaspoon salt
1 cup firmly packed brown sugar
¾ cup egg substitute
¾ cup nonfat buttermilk
1 (8-ounce) can crushed pineapple in juice,
    drained
2 cups grated carrot
⅓ cup raisins
3 tablespoons vegetable oil
2 teaspoons vanilla extract
Vegetable cooking spray
Orange-Cream Cheese Frosting

Combine first 5 ingredients; set aside. Combine brown sugar and next 7 ingredients in a large mixing bowl; stir in dry ingredients, and beat at medium speed of an electric mixer until well blended.

Pour batter into a 13- x 9- x 2-inch pan coated with cooking spray.

Bake at 350° for 30 to 35 minutes or until a wooden pick inserted in center comes out clean. Cool cake completely in pan on a wire rack. Spread Orange-Cream Cheese Frosting over top of cake. Cover and chill. **Yield: 18 servings.**

Orange-Cream Cheese Frosting

½ cup 1% fat cottage cheese
2 teaspoons vanilla extract
1 (8-ounce) package light cream cheese,
    softened
1 teaspoon grated orange rind
1 cup sifted powdered sugar

Position knife blade in food processor bowl; add cottage cheese. Process about 1 minute or until smooth. Add vanilla, cream cheese, and orange rind; process until smooth. Add powdered sugar; pulse 3 to 5 times until mixture is smooth. **Yield: 1½ cups.**

PER SERVING: 207 CALORIES (21% FROM FAT)
FAT 4.8G (SATURATED FAT 1.8G)
PROTEIN 5.4G CARBOHYDRATE 36.1G
CHOLESTEROL 8MG SODIUM 304MG

Pound Cake

(pictured on page 35)

Vegetable cooking spray
½ cup corn oil margarine, softened
1 cup sugar
⅓ cup egg substitute
2½ cups sifted cake flour
½ teaspoon baking powder
¼ teaspoon baking soda
¼ teaspoon salt
1 (8-ounce) carton low-fat vanilla yogurt
1 tablespoon vanilla extract
¾ teaspoon almond extract

Coat the bottom of a 9- x 5- x 3-inch loafpan with cooking spray; dust with flour, and set aside.

Beat margarine at medium speed of an electric mixer until fluffy. Gradually add sugar; beat well. Add egg substitute; beat until blended.

Combine flour and next 3 ingredients; add to creamed mixture alternately with yogurt, beginning and ending with flour mixture. Mix just until blended after each addition. Stir in flavorings.

Spoon batter into prepared pan. Bake at 350° for 1 hour and 5 minutes or until a wooden pick inserted in center comes out clean. Cool in pan on a wire rack 10 minutes; remove from pan, and let cool on wire rack. Serve with ½ cup chopped or sliced fruit. **Yield: 18 (½-inch) servings.**

PER SERVING: 159 CALORIES (30% FROM FAT)
FAT 5.4G (SATURATED FAT 1.1G)
PROTEIN 2.4G CARBOHYDRATE 24.9G
CHOLESTEROL 1MG SODIUM 125MG

Strawberry Shortcake

Strawberry Shortcake

4 cups sliced fresh strawberries
¼ cup sugar
Vegetable cooking spray
¼ cup margarine, softened
⅓ cup sugar
1 large egg, separated
1¾ cups all-purpose flour
1½ teaspoons baking powder
¼ teaspoon salt
¾ cup skim milk
½ teaspoon vanilla extract
1 egg white
2 tablespoons sugar
1½ cups thawed, reduced-calorie frozen
    whipped topping

Combine strawberries and ¼ cup sugar; cover and chill 2 to 3 hours, stirring occasionally.

Coat a 9-inch round cakepan with vegetable cooking spray; dust with flour, and set aside.

Beat margarine at medium speed of an electric mixer until soft; add ⅓ cup sugar, beating well. Add egg yolk, beating just until blended.

Combine flour, baking powder, and salt in a small bowl; add to creamed mixture alternately with milk, beginning and ending with flour mixture. Mix after each addition. Stir in vanilla.

Beat 2 egg whites until foamy. Gradually add 2 tablespoons sugar, one at a time, beating until stiff peaks form. Stir about ½ cup beaten egg white into batter; fold in remaining egg white. Spoon batter into prepared pan.

Bake at 350° for 30 minutes or until a wooden pick inserted in center comes out clean. Let cool in pan on a wire rack 10 minutes. Remove cake from pan; let cool completely on wire rack.

Slice shortcake in half horizontally. Place bottom half, cut side up, on a serving plate.

Drain strawberries, reserving juice; drizzle half of juice over bottom layer. Set aside 1 tablespoon whipped topping. Spread ¾ cup topping over cake layer; arrange half of strawberries over topping. Top with remaining layer, cut side down. Repeat procedure. Dollop with reserved 1 tablespoon whipped topping. **Yield: 9 servings.**

PER SERVING: 260 CALORIES (27% FROM FAT)
FAT 7.9G (SATURATED FAT 1.2G)
PROTEIN 5.1G CARBOHYDRATE 42.9G
CHOLESTEROL 25MG SODIUM 157MG

Chocolate Mint Torte

Vegetable cooking spray
1 (18.5-ounce) package 97% fat-free devil's
    food cake mix
3 egg whites
1¾ cups water
1 (2.6-ounce) package whipped topping mix
⅔ cup skim milk
2 tablespoons green crème de menthe

Coat a 15- x 10- x 1-inch jellyroll pan with cooking spray; line with wax paper, and coat with cooking spray.

Combine cake mix, egg whites, and water in a large mixing bowl; beat at high speed of an electric mixer 2 minutes. Pour batter into prepared pan.

Bake at 350° for 18 to 20 minutes or until a wooden pick inserted in center comes out clean.

Cool in pan on a wire rack 10 minutes. Invert onto wire rack.

Remove wax paper carefully; cool completely. Cut cake crosswise into thirds.

Combine whipped topping mix, milk, and crème de menthe in a mixing bowl; beat at high speed of an electric mixer 4 minutes or until stiff peaks form.

Spread topping between layers, reserving ½ cup. Pipe reserved topping on top of cake. Chill at least 2 hours or freeze. **Yield: 12 servings.**

PER SERVING: 204 CALORIES (13% FROM FAT)
FAT 3.0G (SATURATED FAT 0.0G)
PROTEIN 4.7G CARBOHYDRATE 38.0G
CHOLESTEROL 0MG SODIUM 319MG

Lemon Cheesecake

Lemon Cheesecake

3 cups nonfat yogurt
1 envelope unflavored gelatin
⅓ cup lemon juice
¾ cup sugar
1½ cups 1% low-fat cottage cheese
½ cup light process cream cheese
2 teaspoons grated lemon rind
Graham Cracker Crust
Garnishes: lemon rind curls, fresh mint sprigs

Place colander in a large bowl. Line with 2 layers of cheesecloth or a coffee filter. Spoon yogurt into colander. Cover loosely; chill 24 hours. Discard liquid. Cover; chill yogurt cheese.

Sprinkle gelatin over lemon juice in a small saucepan; let stand 1 minute. Add sugar; cook over low heat, stirring until gelatin dissolves.

Remove from heat, and place in container of a food processor or electric blender. Add cottage cheese; cover and process until smooth. Add cream cheese and grated lemon rind; process until smooth.

Add yogurt cheese, and process until smooth; pour mixture into crust. Cover and chill 8 hours. Garnish, if desired. **Yield: 10 servings.**

Graham Cracker Crust

¾ cup graham cracker crumbs
3 tablespoons reduced-calorie margarine, melted
¼ cup sugar

Combine all ingredients; mix well, and press mixture firmly into a 9-inch springform pan. Bake at 350° for 8 to 10 minutes. Cool. **Yield: one 9-inch crust.**

PER SLICE: 218 CALORIES (22% FROM FAT)
FAT 5.3G (SATURATED FAT 1.9G)
PROTEIN 10.4G CARBOHYDRATE 33.2G
CHOLESTEROL 9MG SODIUM 334MG

Black Forest Cheesecake

(pictured on cover)

¾ cup teddy bear-shaped chocolate graham
   cracker cookies, crushed
Butter-flavored cooking spray
2 (12-ounce) packages nonfat cream cheese,
   softened
1½ cups sugar
¾ cup egg substitute
1 (6-ounce) package semisweet chocolate
   morsels, melted
¼ cup unsweetened cocoa
1½ teaspoons vanilla extract
1 (8-ounce) carton nonfat sour cream
   alternative
1 (21-ounce) can reduced-calorie cherry pie
   filling
½ cup reduced-calorie frozen whipped
   topping, thawed
Garnishes: fresh cherries, mint sprig

Spread cookie crumbs on bottom of a 9-inch springform pan coated with cooking spray; set aside.

Beat cream cheese at high speed of an electric mixer until fluffy; add sugar, beating well. Add egg substitute, mixing well. Add melted chocolate, cocoa, and vanilla, mixing until blended. Stir in sour cream. Pour into prepared pan.

Bake at 300° for 1 hour and 40 minutes. Remove from oven; run a knife around edge of pan to release sides. Let cool completely on a wire rack; cover and chill at least 8 hours.

Remove sides of pan; spread cheesecake with cherry pie filling. Spoon whipped topping in center. Garnish, if desired. **Yield: 12 servings.**

Note: For a creamy-textured cheesecake, bake at 300° for 1 hour and 20 minutes.

PER SLICE: 302 CALORIES (18% FROM FAT)
FAT 6.0G (SATURATED FAT 2.8G)
PROTEIN 12.5G CARBOHYDRATE 47.1G
CHOLESTEROL 13MG SODIUM 406MG

Chocolate-Hazelnut Biscotti

2 large eggs
⅔ cup sugar
1 tablespoon Frangelico or other hazelnut-
   flavored liqueur
2 cups sifted cake flour
1½ teaspoons baking powder
¼ teaspoon salt
1½ tablespoons cocoa
⅔ cup hazelnuts, chopped and toasted
Vegetable cooking spray

Beat eggs at medium speed of an electric mixer until foamy. Gradually add sugar, beating at high speed until mixture is thick and pale. Add liqueur, beating until blended.

Combine flour and next 3 ingredients; fold into egg mixture. Fold in nuts. Cover and chill 30 minutes.

Coat a large cookie sheet with cooking spray. Divide dough into 3 portions, and spoon portions onto cookie sheet 2 inches apart. Shape each portion into an 8- x 1½-inch strip. Cover and chill 30 minutes; reshape, if necessary.

Bake at 375° for 20 minutes or until lightly browned. Remove to wire racks to cool. Cut diagonally into ½-inch-thick slices. Lay slices flat on cookie sheet. Bake at 375° for 5 minutes; turn slices over, and bake 5 additional minutes. Remove to wire racks to cool. **Yield: 3½ dozen.**

PER COOKIE: 47 CALORIES (26% FROM FAT)
FAT 1.4G (SATURATED FAT 0.2G)
PROTEIN 1.0G CARBOHYDRATE 7.8G
CHOLESTEROL 11MG SODIUM 17MG

Oatmeal-Raisin Cookies

Oatmeal-Raisin Cookies

¼ cup margarine, softened
½ cup sugar
½ cup firmly packed brown sugar
½ cup egg substitute
2 teaspoons vanilla extract
¾ cup all-purpose flour
¼ teaspoon baking soda
⅛ teaspoon salt
1½ cups quick-cooking oats, uncooked
½ cup raisins
Vegetable cooking spray

Beat margarine at medium speed of an electric mixer. Gradually add sugars, beating well. Add egg substitute and vanilla; mix well.

Combine flour and next 3 ingredients. Gradually add to margarine mixture, mixing well. Stir in raisins.

Drop dough by 2 teaspoonfuls onto cookie sheets coated with cooking spray.

Bake at 350° for 10 to 12 minutes or until lightly browned. Remove to wire racks to cool.
Yield: 3 dozen.

PER COOKIE: 65 CALORIES (21% FROM FAT)
FAT 1.5G (SATURATED FAT 0.3G)
PROTEIN 1.2G CARBOHYDRATE 11.7G
CHOLESTEROL 0MG SODIUM 27MG

Lighten Up Cookies

When making cookies with regular or reduced-calorie margarine, be sure to use stick-type margarine, not a spread. If you are using 100 percent corn oil margarine, the dough may be softer than with other margarines and may need to be chilled if the cookies will be sliced or shaped.

Raspberry-Cherry Cobbler

1 (16-ounce) package frozen unsweetened raspberries, thawed
1 (16-ounce) package frozen no-sugar-added pitted dark sweet cherries, thawed
1 cup sugar
¼ cup all-purpose flour
1 tablespoon lemon juice
⅛ teaspoon ground cinnamon
Vegetable cooking spray
2 cups all-purpose flour
1 tablespoon baking powder
1 teaspoon baking soda
1 teaspoon salt
2 tablespoons sugar
¼ cup reduced-calorie margarine
¾ cup plain nonfat yogurt
¼ cup evaporated skimmed milk

Combine first 6 ingredients, and spoon into an 11- x 7- x 1½-inch baking dish coated with cooking spray.

Combine 2 cups flour and next 4 ingredients in a large bowl; cut in margarine with a pastry blender until mixture is crumbly. Add yogurt and milk, stirring with a fork until dry ingredients are moistened.

Turn dough out onto a lightly floured surface, and knead about 10 times. Roll dough to ½-inch thickness; cut 12 rounds using a 2-inch cutter. Cut 6 diamonds from remaining dough.

Arrange rounds and diamond shapes on top of fruit mixture.

Bake at 425° for 20 to 25 minutes or until bubbly and golden. Remove from oven; lightly coat each biscuit with cooking spray. **Yield: 12 servings.**

PER SERVING: 225 CALORIES (11% FROM FAT)
FAT 2.7G (SATURATED FAT 0.4G)
PROTEIN 4.4G CARBOHYDRATE 47.1G
CHOLESTEROL 0MG SODIUM 403MG

Buttermilk Pie

(pictured on page 35)

⅔ cup sugar
¼ cup cornstarch
2½ cups nonfat buttermilk
3 tablespoons light process cream cheese
⅔ cup egg substitute
1 teaspoon grated lemon rind
2 tablespoons lemon juice
½ teaspoon lemon extract
Light Pastry
3 egg whites
½ teaspoon cream of tartar
1 tablespoon sugar
⅛ teaspoon lemon extract
Garnishes: lemon rind curls, fresh mint sprigs

Combine ⅔ cup sugar and cornstarch in a heavy saucepan; gradually stir in buttermilk. Add cream cheese, and cook over medium heat, stirring constantly, until mixture thickens and comes to a boil. Boil, stirring constantly, 1 minute.

Stir about one-fourth of hot mixture gradually into egg substitute; add to remaining hot mixture, stirring constantly. Cook over low heat, stirring constantly, 2 minutes.

Remove from heat; stir in lemon rind, juice, and ½ teaspoon lemon extract. Spoon into baked pastry shell.

Beat egg whites and cream of tartar at medium speed of an electric mixer until foamy. Gradually add 1 tablespoon sugar, beating until stiff peaks form. Stir in ⅛ teaspoon lemon extract. Spread meringue over filling, sealing to edge.

Bake at 325° for 25 to 28 minutes. Garnish, if desired. **Yield: 8 servings.**

Light Pastry

1¼ cups all-purpose flour
⅓ cup corn oil margarine
3 tablespoons cold water

Place flour in a bowl; cut in margarine with a pastry blender until mixture is crumbly. Sprinkle cold water (1 tablespoon at a time) evenly over surface; stir with a fork until dry ingredients are moistened.

Shape dough into a ball; gently press between 2 sheets of heavy-duty plastic wrap into a 4-inch circle. Chill 15 minutes.

Roll dough into an 11-inch circle; freeze 5 minutes. Remove top sheet of plastic wrap, and invert into a 9-inch pieplate. Remove plastic wrap. Fold edges under and crimp; prick bottom and sides with a fork.

Bake at 425° for 15 minutes or until golden. Cool on a wire rack. **Yield: one (9-inch) pastry shell.**

PER SERVING: 285 CALORIES (28% FROM FAT)
FAT 8.9G (SATURATED FAT 2.3G)
PROTEIN 8.8G CARBOHYDRATE 42.0G
CHOLESTEROL 6MG SODIUM 253MG

Treat Yourself to Dessert

• Fresh fruit, loaded with vitamins, minerals, and fiber, is always a good dessert choice.
• Angel food cake contains no fat and is a smart selection for healthy eating.
• Frozen fruit sorbet or nonfat frozen yogurt is a delicious substitution for ice cream.

Flaky Apple Turnovers

Flaky Apple Turnovers

2¼ cups peeled, chopped cooking apples
　　(¾ pound)
1½ teaspoons lemon juice
¼ cup sugar
1 tablespoon all-purpose flour
½ teaspoon ground cinnamon
⅛ teaspoon salt
⅛ teaspoon ground nutmeg
7 sheets frozen phyllo pastry, thawed
Vegetable cooking spray

Combine apples and lemon juice in a bowl; toss gently. Add sugar and next 4 ingredients; toss well, and set mixture aside.

Keep phyllo covered with a slightly damp towel until ready for use. Working with 1 phyllo sheet at a time, cut each sheet lengthwise into 4 (3½-inch-wide) strips; lightly spray with cooking spray. Stack 2 strips, one on top of the other.

Spoon 1 tablespoon apple mixture onto each stack; spread to within 1 inch of each end. Fold left bottom corner over mixture, forming a triangle. Keep folding back and forth into a triangle to end of stack. Repeat with remaining ingredients.

Place triangles, seam side down, on a baking sheet coated with cooking spray. Lightly spray tops of triangles with cooking spray.

Bake at 400° for 15 minutes or until golden. Serve warm. **Yield: 14 turnovers.**

PER TURNOVER: 60 CALORIES (18% FROM FAT)
FAT 1.2G (SATURATED FAT 0.1G)
PROTEIN 0.8G CARBOHYDRATE 11.7G
CHOLESTEROL 0MG SODIUM 67MG

Old-Fashioned Banana Pudding

½ cup sugar
3 tablespoons cornstarch
⅓ cup water
1 (12-ounce) can evaporated skimmed milk
⅓ cup egg substitute
½ cup fat-free sour cream
1 teaspoon vanilla extract
22 vanilla wafers
3 medium bananas, sliced
3 egg whites
¼ teaspoon cream of tartar
1 tablespoon sugar

Combine ½ cup sugar and cornstarch in a heavy saucepan; stir in next 3 ingredients. Cook over medium heat, stirring constantly, until mixture boils. Boil, stirring constantly, 1 minute. Remove from heat; fold in sour cream and vanilla.

Place a layer of wafers in bottom of a 1½-quart baking dish. Spoon one-third of pudding over wafers; top with half of bananas. Repeat layers, ending with pudding; place wafers around edge.

Beat egg whites and cream of tartar at medium speed of an electric mixer until foamy. Gradually add 1 tablespoon sugar; beat until stiff peaks form. Spread meringue over pudding, sealing to edge.

Bake at 325° for 25 to 28 minutes. **Yield: 10 (½-cup) servings.**

PER SERVING: 172 CALORIES (12% FROM FAT)
FAT 2.2G (SATURATED FAT 0.1G)
PROTEIN 6.0G CARBOHYDRATE 32.2G
CHOLESTEROL 1MG SODIUM 112MG

Peach Sherbet

1 (8-ounce) carton plain low-fat yogurt
½ cup orange juice
⅓ cup honey
2 cups peeled, sliced ripe peaches or 2 cups frozen peaches, partially thawed

Combine all ingredients in container of an electric blender or food processor. Cover; process until peaches are finely chopped. Pour into an 8-inch square pan; freeze until almost firm.

Remove from freezer; break into chunks, and place in blender container; process until fluffy but not thawed. Return mixture to pan; freeze until firm. Let stand at room temperature 10 minutes before serving. **Yield: 6 (½-cup) servings.**

PER SERVING: 115 CALORIES (5% FROM FAT)
FAT 0.6G (SATURATED FAT 0.4G)
PROTEIN 2.6G CARBOHYDRATE 26.7G
CHOLESTEROL 2MG SODIUM 27MG

Banana Yogurt Ice Milk

1 envelope unflavored gelatin
3 tablespoons water
1 cup mashed ripe banana
1 cup evaporated skimmed milk
1 (8-ounce) carton plain low-fat yogurt
3 tablespoons honey
1 kiwifruit, peeled and thinly sliced
¼ cup blueberries
¼ cup raspberries

Sprinkle gelatin over water in a saucepan; let stand 1 minute. Cook over medium heat, stirring until gelatin dissolves; remove from heat.

Combine banana and next 3 ingredients. Stir into gelatin. Spoon into an 8-inch square pan; freeze until firm.

Remove from freezer; break frozen mixture into chunks. Spoon into a bowl; beat at medium speed of an electric mixer until smooth. Return mixture to pan; freeze until firm. Let stand at room temperature 10 minutes.

Serve with kiwifruit, blueberries, and raspberries. **Yield: 7 (½-cup) servings.**

PER SERVING: 120 CALORIES (6% FROM FAT)
FAT 0.8G (SATURATED FAT 0.4G)
PROTEIN 5.9G CARBOHYDRATE 23.8G
CHOLESTEROL 3MG SODIUM 67MG

Banana Yogurt Ice Milk

Fresh Strawberry Ice Milk

(pictured on page 35)

4 cups fresh strawberries
1½ cups sugar, divided
3 cups skim milk
2 envelopes unflavored gelatin
½ cup egg substitute
2 (12-ounce) cans evaporated skimmed milk
1½ tablespoons vanilla extract
3 drops of red food coloring
Garnish: 16 whole fresh strawberries

Place strawberries in container of an electric blender or food processor, and process just until chopped. Sprinkle strawberries with ½ cup sugar, and set aside.

Combine remaining 1 cup sugar and skim milk in a saucepan; sprinkle gelatin over mixture, and let stand 1 minute. Cook mixture over medium heat, stirring constantly, until sugar and gelatin dissolve. Gradually stir in egg substitute; cook mixture 1 minute. Remove mixture from heat and chill.

Stir in chopped strawberries, evaporated skimmed milk, vanilla, and food coloring. Pour into container of a 1-gallon hand-turned or electric freezer.

Freeze according to manufacturer's instructions. Pack ice milk with additional ice and rock salt; let stand 1 hour before serving (ice milk will be soft). Garnish, if desired. **Yield: 16 (1-cup) servings.**

PER SERVING: 143 CALORIES (2% FROM FAT)
FAT 0.3G (SATURATED FAT 0.1G)
PROTEIN 6.5G CARBOHYDRATE 28.7G
CHOLESTEROL 3MG SODIUM 86MG

Cranberries Jubilee

Cranberries Jubilee

1 (12-ounce) package fresh cranberries
1 (10.25-ounce) jar reduced-sugar strawberry jam
1 teaspoon grated orange rind
⅓ cup brandy
2 tablespoons brandy
7 cups vanilla-flavored low-fat frozen yogurt

Combine first 4 ingredients in a saucepan. Bring to a boil over medium heat; cook 5 minutes, stirring constantly, or until cranberries pop and sauce begins to thicken (do not overcook). Remove from heat, and let cool slightly.

Place 2 tablespoons brandy in a small, long-handled saucepan; heat just until warm (do not boil). Remove from heat. Ignite brandy, and pour over cranberries; stir until flames die down. Serve immediately over frozen yogurt. **Yield: 14 (½-cup) servings.**

PER SERVING: 124 CALORIES (12% FROM FAT)
FAT 1.7G (SATURATED FAT 1.2G)
PROTEIN 2.6G CARBOHYDRATE 25.4G
CHOLESTEROL 8MG SODIUM 30MG

Fish & Shellfish

Low in fat and calories and rich in protein, fish and shellfish offer many tasty and healthful options. And for an added bonus—they're easy to prepare and quick to cook.

Crab Cakes, Breaded Catfish with Creole Sauce, Fillets Tomatillo

Crab-and-Mushroom Casserole, Crab-and-Shrimp Étouffée, Baked Oysters Italiano

Steamed Fish and Vegetables, Poached Fish with Greek Sauce, Barbecued Shrimp

Blackened Red Snapper, Peppered Snapper with Creamy Dill Sauce

Grilled Marinated Grouper (page 53)

Breaded Catfish with Creole Sauce

Breaded Catfish with Creole Sauce

½ cup yellow cornmeal
¼ teaspoon pepper
2 tablespoons evaporated skimmed milk
4 (4-ounce) farm-raised catfish fillets
Olive oil-flavored vegetable cooking spray
Creole Sauce

Combine cornmeal and pepper; set aside. Pour milk into a shallow dish. Dip fillets in milk; dredge in cornmeal mixture.

Place fish on a baking sheet coated with cooking spray. Spray each fillet lightly with cooking spray.

Bake at 425° for 10 minutes or until fish flakes easily when tested with a fork. Broil fish 3 inches from heat (with electric oven door partially opened) 1 minute or until browned. Serve fish with Creole Sauce. **Yield: 4 servings.**

Creole Sauce

Olive oil-flavored vegetable cooking spray
1 teaspoon reduced-calorie margarine
¾ cup chopped onion
½ cup chopped celery
2 cloves garlic, minced
1 cup coarsely chopped tomato
1 cup sliced fresh okra
½ cup chopped green pepper
½ teaspoon dried basil
½ teaspoon dried oregano
½ teaspoon dried thyme
¼ teaspoon salt
¼ teaspoon ground red pepper
¼ teaspoon freshly ground black pepper
1 (10½-ounce) can ready-to-serve, no-salt-added chicken broth
1 (8-ounce) can no-salt-added tomato sauce
Dash of hot sauce

Coat a large nonstick skillet with cooking spray; place skillet over medium-high heat. Add margarine, onion, celery, and garlic; cook, stirring constantly, until vegetables are tender. Add tomato and remaining ingredients; bring to a boil. Reduce heat, and simmer, uncovered, 20 minutes, stirring occasionally. **Yield: 3 cups.**

PER SERVING: 267 CALORIES (23% FROM FAT)
FAT 6.8G (SATURATED FAT 1.3G)
PROTEIN 25.0G CARBOHYDRATE 26.3G
CHOLESTEROL 66MG SODIUM 275MG

Grilled Marinated Grouper

(pictured on page 51)

1 teaspoon grated lemon rind
⅓ cup fresh lemon juice
2 teaspoons prepared horseradish
1 teaspoon dried Italian seasoning
½ teaspoon salt
¼ teaspoon pepper
1 clove garlic, halved
1 pound grouper fillet or other lean white fish, cut into 4 pieces
Vegetable cooking spray

Combine first 7 ingredients in container of an electric blender or food processor; cover and process 20 seconds. Arrange fish in a 13- x 9- x 2-inch baking dish. Pour marinade over fish, turning to coat both sides; cover and marinate in refrigerator 4 hours.

Place fish in a wire basket coated with cooking spray. Cook, covered with grill lid, over medium-hot coals (350° to 400°) 7 to 8 minutes on each side or until fish flakes easily when tested with a fork. **Yield: 4 servings.**

PER SERVING: 111 CALORIES (11% FROM FAT)
FAT 1.3G (SATURATED FAT 0.3G)
PROTEIN 21.4G CARBOHYDRATE 2.8G
CHOLESTEROL 40MG SODIUM 341MG

Steamed Fish and Vegetables

Steamed Fish and Vegetables

4 small round red potatoes
2 (4-ounce) grouper fillets or other lean
    white fish
2 small yellow squash
8 medium okra
½ pound fresh or frozen green beans
1 cup sweet red pepper slices
½ cup sliced onion
1 tablespoon reduced-calorie margarine
½ teaspoon salt-free herb-and-spice blend

Place potatoes in a vegetable steamer over boiling water; cover and steam 10 minutes. Add fish and next 3 ingredients; cover and steam 10 minutes. Add red pepper slices and onion.

Dot with margarine, and sprinkle with herb-and-spice blend; cover and steam 5 minutes. **Yield: 2 servings.**

PER SERVING: 316 CALORIES (16% FROM FAT)
FAT 5.5G (SATURATED FAT 0.9G)
PROTEIN 29.2G CARBOHYDRATE 40.1G
CHOLESTEROL 41MG SODIUM 126MG

Poached Fish with Greek Sauce

2 tablespoons chopped onion
2 sprigs fresh parsley
½ bay leaf
⅛ teaspoon salt
4 whole peppercorns
½ cup Chablis or other dry white wine
½ cup water
4 (4-ounce) skinned flounder fillets or other lean white fish
Greek Sauce

Combine first 7 ingredients in an 11- x 7- x 1½-inch baking dish. Cover with heavy-duty plastic wrap; fold back a small corner of wrap for steam to escape.

Microwave at HIGH 5 minutes or until boiling. Uncover; arrange fillets in liquid with thickest portion to outside of dish.

Cover and microwave at HIGH 4 minutes, giving dish a half-turn after 2 minutes. Cook until fish turns opaque. Let stand, covered, 3 to 5 minutes. Fish is done if it flakes easily when tested with a fork. Remove bay leaf.

Remove to a serving dish, reserving liquid. Serve with Greek Sauce. **Yield: 4 servings.**

Greek Sauce

¼ cup reduced-fat mayonnaise
¼ cup plain low-fat yogurt
¼ cup minced fresh parsley
2 tablespoons lemon juice
⅛ teaspoon fresh ground pepper
⅛ teaspoon garlic powder
2 tablespoons reserved poaching liquid

Combine all ingredients in a small bowl; stir well. **Yield: ¾ cup.**

PER SERVING: 138 CALORIES (17% FROM FAT)
FAT 2.6G (SATURATED FAT 0.5G)
PROTEIN 21.5G CARBOHYDRATE 6.2G
CHOLESTEROL 59MG SODIUM 279MG

Fillets Tomatillo

1 cup finely chopped fresh tomatillo (4 large tomatillos)
¼ cup finely chopped onion
¼ cup finely chopped celery
2 tablespoons chopped green pepper
1 clove garlic, minced
2 teaspoons olive oil
¼ cup clam juice or chicken broth
2 tablespoons canned chopped green chiles
2 tablespoons lime juice
½ teaspoon chopped fresh cilantro
½ teaspoon ground cumin
¼ teaspoon dried oregano
⅛ teaspoon salt
⅛ teaspoon ground red pepper
4 (4-ounce) orange roughy fillets
Vegetable cooking spray

Cook first 5 ingredients in olive oil in a medium skillet over medium-high heat, stirring constantly, 5 minutes.

Add clam juice and next 7 ingredients; cover, reduce heat, and simmer 15 minutes, stirring occasionally. Remove from heat, and keep warm.

Arrange fish in a grill basket coated with cooking spray. Cook, covered with grill lid, over medium-hot coals (350° to 400°) 7 to 8 minutes on each side or until fish flakes easily with a fork. Serve fillets with tomatillo mixture. **Yield: 4 servings.**

PER SERVING: 124 CALORIES (27% FROM FAT)
FAT 3.7G (SATURATED FAT 0.3G)
PROTEIN 17.4G CARBOHYDRATE 4.8G
CHOLESTEROL 23MG SODIUM 193MG

Blackened Red Snapper

Vegetable cooking spray
1 tablespoon olive oil
¼ cup minced onion
2 cloves garlic, minced
½ tablespoon paprika
¼ teaspoon ground white pepper
¼ teaspoon ground red pepper
¼ teaspoon black pepper
¼ teaspoon dried oregano
4 (5-ounce) skinned red snapper fillets

Coat a nonstick skillet with cooking spray; place over medium-high heat until hot. Add olive oil, onion, and garlic; cook, stirring constantly, until onion is tender.

Stir in paprika and next 4 ingredients; set aside to cool. Spread cooled spice mixture on both sides of fish fillets.

Place fish on rack coated with cooking spray; place rack in a broiler pan. Broil 3 inches from heat (with electric oven door partially opened) 7 to 9 minutes or until fish flakes easily when tested with a fork (fish will be lightly charred). **Yield: 4 servings.**

PER SERVING: 183 CALORIES (28% FROM FAT)
FAT 5.6G (SATURATED FAT 0.9G)
PROTEIN 29.5G CARBOHYDRATE 2.2G
CHOLESTEROL 52MG SODIUM 64MG

Peppered Snapper with Creamy Dill Sauce

4 (4-ounce) red snapper fillets
2 teaspoons olive oil, divided
2 tablespoons coarsely ground pepper
Vegetable cooking spray
2 cups hot cooked rice (cooked without salt or fat)
Creamy Dill Sauce

Brush snapper on both sides with 1 teaspoon olive oil; sprinkle with pepper, and gently press into fish. Cover and let stand 15 minutes.

Coat a large nonstick skillet with cooking spray; add remaining 1 teaspoon olive oil, and place over medium heat. Cook fillets on both sides 3 to 5 minutes or until fish flakes easily when tested with a fork. Remove from heat; keep warm.

Spoon rice evenly onto serving plates; top each with a fillet and Creamy Dill Sauce. Serve immediately. **Yield: 4 servings.**

Creamy Dill Sauce

1 (10-ounce) container refrigerated reduced-calorie Alfredo sauce
2 tablespoons Chablis or other dry white wine
1 teaspoon dried dill

Combine all ingredients in a small heavy saucepan; cook, stirring constantly, over medium heat until thoroughly heated. Remove from heat; keep warm. **Yield: 1 cup.**

PER SERVING: 389 CALORIES (28% FROM FAT)
FAT 11.9G (SATURATED FAT 6.8G)
PROTEIN 31.7G CARBOHYDRATE 33.9G
CHOLESTEROL 72MG SODIUM 1825MG

Red Snapper Veracruz

Vegetable cooking spray
½ cup chopped green pepper
¼ cup chopped onion
2 cloves garlic, minced
1½ cups chopped, peeled tomato (about 2)
2 tablespoons chopped green chiles, drained
1 tablespoon chopped fresh cilantro or parsley
¼ teaspoon salt
¼ teaspoon hot sauce
Dash of ground white pepper
4 (4-ounce) red snapper fillets
2 teaspoons margarine, melted

Coat a nonstick skillet with cooking spray; place over medium-high heat until hot. Add green pepper, onion, and garlic; cook, stirring constantly, until tender.

Stir in tomato and next 5 ingredients; cook, stirring frequently, until thoroughly heated.

Brush fish with margarine; place in a grill basket coated with cooking spray. Cook, covered with grill lid, over medium-hot coals (350° to 400°) 5 minutes on each side or until fish flakes easily when tested with a fork. Serve fish with tomato mixture. **Yield: 4 servings.**

PER SERVING: 154 CALORIES (23% FROM FAT)
FAT 4.0G (SATURATED FAT 0.7G)
PROTEIN 23.4G CARBOHYDRATE 5.7G
CHOLESTEROL 40MG SODIUM 226MG

Poached Salmon with Horseradish Sauce

4 cups water
1 lemon, sliced
1 carrot, sliced
1 stalk celery, sliced
1 teaspoon peppercorns
4 (4-ounce) salmon steaks
Horseradish Sauce

Combine first 5 ingredients in a large skillet; bring to a boil over medium-high heat. Cover, reduce heat, and simmer 10 minutes.

Add salmon steaks; cover and simmer 10 minutes. Remove skillet from heat; let stand 8 minutes. Remove salmon steaks to serving plate; serve with Horseradish Sauce. **Yield: 4 servings.**

Horseradish Sauce
¼ cup nonfat mayonnaise
¼ cup plain nonfat yogurt
2 teaspoons prepared horseradish
1½ teaspoons lemon juice
1½ teaspoons chopped fresh chives

Combine all ingredients in a small bowl; cover and chill. **Yield: ½ cup.**

Note: Because salmon is high in omega-3 fatty acid (a polyunsaturated fat in fish with dark, moist flesh), this recipe derives more than 30 percent of total calories per serving from fat.

PER SERVING: 205 CALORIES (41% FROM FAT)
FAT 9.4G (SATURATED FAT 1.7G)
PROTEIN 24.1G CARBOHYDRATE 4.5G
CHOLESTEROL 74MG SODIUM 259MG

Salmon-Pesto Vermicelli

1 cup firmly packed fresh basil leaves
¼ cup commercial oil-free Italian dressing
2 tablespoons water
3 cloves garlic, crushed
1 (1-pound) salmon fillet
¼ teaspoon cracked pepper
Vegetable cooking spray
4 cups cooked vermicelli (cooked without salt or fat)
6 lemon wedges (optional)

Combine first 4 ingredients in food processor bowl fitted with knife blade. Process 2 minutes, scraping sides of bowl occasionally. Set aside.

Sprinkle fish with pepper, and place, skin side down, on a broiler pan coated with cooking spray. Broil 6 inches from heat (with electric oven door partially opened) 5 minutes.

Turn fish over carefully, and broil (with electric oven door partially opened) 4 minutes or until fish flakes easily when tested with a fork. Remove from pan; cool. Remove and discard skin; break fish into bite-size pieces.

Combine fish, basil mixture, and vermicelli in a large bowl; toss gently. Serve with lemon wedges, if desired. **Yield: 6 servings.**

PER SERVING: 265 CALORIES (24% FROM FAT)
FAT 7.0G (SATURATED FAT 1.2G)
PROTEIN 20.3G CARBOHYDRATE 28.5G
CHOLESTEROL 49MG SODIUM 146MG

Seared Tuna Steaks on Mixed Greens with Lemon-Basil Vinaigrette

4 (4-ounce) tuna steaks
1 tablespoon reduced-sodium Cajun seasoning
Vegetable cooking spray
8 cups mixed salad greens
Lemon-Basil Vinaigrette
Garnish: finely chopped sweet red pepper

Sprinkle tuna evenly with seasoning.

Coat food rack with cooking spray; place rack on grill over medium-hot coals (350° to 400°). Place tuna on rack.

Cook, covered with grill lid, 5 minutes on each side or until done.

Cover and chill at least 8 hours.

Combine salad greens and half of Lemon-Basil Vinaigrette; arrange on 4 plates. Top each with a tuna steak, and drizzle evenly with remaining vinaigrette. Garnish, if desired. **Yield: 4 servings.**

Lemon-Basil Vinaigrette

2 lemons, peeled, sectioned, and finely chopped
2 tablespoons white wine vinegar
1 tablespoon vegetable oil
1 tablespoon fresh basil, finely chopped
¼ teaspoon cracked black pepper
¼ teaspoon hot sauce

Combine all ingredients in a jar. Cover tightly, and shake vigorously. **Yield: ½ cup.**

PER SERVING: 189 CALORIES (24% FROM FAT)
FAT 5.1G (SATURATED FAT 0.3G)
PROTEIN 28.4G CARBOHYDRATE 7.7G
CHOLESTEROL 51MG SODIUM 59MG

Crab Cakes

2 egg whites, lightly beaten
2 tablespoons reduced-calorie mayonnaise
2 teaspoons chopped fresh parsley
1¼ teaspoons Old Bay seasoning
1 teaspoon reduced-sodium Worcestershire sauce
1 teaspoon dry mustard
¼ teaspoon pepper
½ cup soft breadcrumbs
1 pound fresh, lump crabmeat, drained
Olive oil-flavored vegetable cooking spray

Combine first 7 ingredients. Stir in soft breadcrumbs and crabmeat, and shape into 8 (2½-inch) patties. Place on a baking sheet lined with wax paper; chill 30 minutes.

Coat a large nonstick skillet with cooking spray; place over medium-high heat until hot. Add crab cakes, and cook 3 minutes on each side or until browned. **Yield: 4 servings.**

Note: The crab cakes may be broiled on a nonstick baking sheet coated with cooking spray. Broil on one side for 5 minutes or until golden.

PER SERVING: 166 CALORIES (25% FROM FAT)
FAT 4.6G (SATURATED FAT 0.6G)
PROTEIN 25.4G CARBOHYDRATE 4.2G
CHOLESTEROL 116MG SODIUM 613MG

Preparing Fish

• Cook seafood within 24 hours of purchase. If a fish smells "fishy" or like ammonia, don't buy it.

• To keep grilled fish from sticking, spray the grill basket or rack with vegetable cooking spray before grilling.

• The amount of grilling time depends on the kind of fish and its thickness. A good guide is to allow 6 to 12 minutes per inch of thickness.

Crab Cakes

Crab-and-Mushroom Casserole

¼ cup finely chopped onion
¼ cup finely chopped celery
¼ cup finely chopped green pepper
2 tablespoons reduced-calorie margarine,
    melted
1 pound fresh mushrooms, sliced
¼ cup all-purpose flour
2 cups low-sodium chicken broth
½ cup egg substitute
1 pound fresh crabmeat, drained and flaked
1 tablespoon salt-free herb-and-spice blend
¾ teaspoon salt
⅛ teaspoon ground ginger
Vegetable cooking spray
¼ cup (1 ounce) shredded reduced-fat sharp
    Cheddar cheese

Cook onion, celery, and green pepper in margarine in a large skillet, stirring constantly, until tender. Add mushrooms, and cook 10 minutes.

Add flour, stirring until smooth. Cook 1 minute, stirring constantly. Gradually add chicken broth; cook over medium heat, stirring constantly, until mixture is thickened and bubbly.

Stir one-fourth of hot mixture into egg substitute; add to remaining hot mixture, stirring constantly. Stir in crabmeat and next 3 ingredients.

Spoon mixture into an 11- x 7- x 1½-inch baking dish coated with cooking spray.

Bake at 350° for 35 minutes; sprinkle with cheese, and bake 5 additional minutes. **Yield: 6 servings.**

PER SERVING: 179 CALORIES (28% FROM FAT)
FAT 5.6G (SATURATED FAT 1.3G)
PROTEIN 21.0G CARBOHYDRATE 11.6G
CHOLESTEROL 74MG SODIUM 628MG

Crab-and-Shrimp Étouffée

2 pounds unpeeled medium-size fresh shrimp
⅔ cup chopped onion
¼ cup chopped green pepper
¼ cup chopped celery
3 cloves garlic, minced
2 tablespoons reduced-calorie margarine,
    melted
⅔ cup no-salt-added chicken broth
⅓ cup white wine
1 tablespoon no-salt-added tomato paste
¼ cup chopped green onions
2 tablespoons chopped fresh parsley
2 teaspoons low-sodium Worcestershire sauce
¼ teaspoon salt
¼ teaspoon pepper
⅛ teaspoon hot sauce
1½ tablespoons cornstarch
⅓ cup no-salt-added chicken broth
12 ounces fresh crabmeat, drained and flaked
2 cups hot cooked rice (cooked without salt
    or fat)

Peel and devein shrimp; set aside. Cook ⅔ cup chopped onion and next 3 ingredients in margarine in a large skillet until tender.

Stir in ⅔ cup chicken broth and next 8 ingredients. Add shrimp; cover and simmer 5 minutes, stirring occasionally.

Combine cornstarch and ⅓ cup chicken broth; add to shrimp mixture. Cook, stirring constantly, until mixture boils; boil 1 minute, stirring constantly.

Stir in crabmeat, and cook until thoroughly heated. Serve over hot cooked rice. **Yield: 6 servings.**

PER SERVING: 297 CALORIES (17% FROM FAT)
FAT 5.5G (SATURATED FAT 0.8G)
PROTEIN 35.6G CARBOHYDRATE 23.7G
CHOLESTEROL 224MG SODIUM 464MG

Baked Oysters Italiano

Baked Oysters Italiano

Rock salt
3 tablespoons commercial oil-free Italian
    dressing
2 teaspoons lemon juice
¼ teaspoon hot sauce
2 tablespoons Italian-seasoned
    breadcrumbs
1 tablespoon grated Parmesan cheese
⅛ teaspoon garlic powder
⅛ teaspoon dried Italian seasoning
12 medium-size fresh raw oysters on the
    half shell
1 tablespoon minced fresh parsley

Sprinkle a thin layer of rock salt in a shallow baking pan.

Combine Italian dressing, lemon juice, and hot sauce; set aside. Combine breadcrumbs and next 3 ingredients; set aside.

Place oysters (in shells) over rock salt. Sprinkle each oyster evenly with Italian dressing mixture and breadcrumb mixture.

Bake at 425° for 6 to 8 minutes or until edges of oysters begin to curl. Sprinkle with fresh parsley. **Yield: 12 oysters.**

PER OYSTER: 18 CALORIES (25% FROM FAT)
FAT 0.5G (SATURATED FAT 0.2G)
PROTEIN 1.4G CARBOHYDRATE 2.0G
CHOLESTEROL 8MG SODIUM 98MG

Grilled Orange Scallops with Cilantro-Lime Vinaigrette

Grilled Orange Scallops with Cilantro-Lime Vinaigrette

1 cup orange juice
3 tablespoons chopped fresh basil
18 sea scallops
1 head Bibb lettuce
4 cups mixed baby lettuces
Cilantro-Lime Vinaigrette
30 yellow pear-shaped cherry tomatoes
30 red pear-shaped cherry tomatoes
2 cucumbers, cut into thin strips
Garnishes: fresh basil sprigs, thin orange rind
   strips

Combine orange juice and basil in a shallow dish; add scallops, tossing to coat.

Cover dish, and chill about 1 hour. Uncover and drain, discarding marinade.

Cook scallops, covered with grill lid, over hot coals (400° to 500°) 3 to 5 minutes on each side or until done.

Combine lettuces in a bowl; drizzle with Cilantro-Lime Vinaigrette, and toss gently.

Arrange lettuces on individual plates, and top with scallops, tomatoes, and cucumber. Garnish, if desired. Serve immediately. **Yield: 6 servings.**

Cilantro-Lime Vinaigrette

¼ cup sugar
¼ cup extra-virgin olive oil
2 tablespoons lime juice
2 tablespoons rice wine vinegar
1 clove garlic, minced
1 shallot, minced
1½ teaspoons fresh cilantro leaves, finely
   chopped

Combine all ingredients in a jar. Cover tightly, and shake mixture vigorously. **Yield: ¾ cup.**

Note: Scallops may be grilled directly on grill rack or, if rack openings are too large, in a grill basket or threaded on skewers.

PER SERVING: 268 CALORIES (29% FROM FAT)
FAT 8.5G (SATURATED FAT 1.1G)
PROTEIN 25.4G CARBOHYDRATE 23.7G
CHOLESTEROL 45MG SODIUM 240MG

Broiled Marinated Shrimp

2 tablespoons sliced green onions
2 cloves garlic, minced
Vegetable cooking spray
¾ cup ready-to-serve, no-salt-added chicken
   broth
3 tablespoons reduced-fat creamy peanut
   butter spread
1 tablespoon reduced-sodium soy sauce
1 tablespoon lemon juice
1 teaspoon chili powder
1 teaspoon brown sugar
½ teaspoon ground ginger
1 pound unpeeled large fresh shrimp

Cook green onions and garlic in a skillet coated with cooking spray over medium heat, stirring constantly, about 3 minutes.

Add chicken broth and next 6 ingredients, stirring until smooth. Reduce heat; simmer 10 minutes, stirring often. Remove from heat; cool.

Peel and devein shrimp, leaving tails attached. Place shrimp in sauce; turn to coat. Cover and chill 1 hour. Remove from sauce; discard sauce. Thread shrimp onto skewers.

Broil 6 inches from heat (with electric oven door partially opened) 5 minutes on each side or until shrimp turn pink. **Yield: 4 servings.**

PER SERVING: 106 CALORIES (27% FROM FAT)
FAT 3.2G (SATURATED FAT 0.6G)
PROTEIN 15.1G CARBOHYDRATE 4.3G
CHOLESTEROL 124MG SODIUM 234MG

Barbecued Shrimp

Barbecued Shrimp

Olive oil-flavored vegetable cooking spray
¼ cup diced onion
1 tablespoon brown sugar
1 tablespoon dry mustard
¼ teaspoon garlic powder
1 tablespoon white vinegar
½ cup reduced-calorie ketchup
Dash of hot sauce
2 tablespoons fresh rosemary, chopped
24 unpeeled jumbo fresh shrimp
1 lemon, cut into wedges

Coat a nonstick skillet with cooking spray; place over medium-high heat until hot. Add onion, and cook, stirring constantly, until tender; remove from heat.

Add brown sugar and next 6 ingredients; stir until well blended. Let stand 2 to 3 hours.

Peel and devein shrimp; place in a shallow dish. Pour marinade over shrimp, turning to coat both sides. Cover and chill 1 hour.

Soak 4 (8-inch) wooden skewers in water 30 minutes. Thread tail and neck of six shrimp on each skewer so shrimp will lie flat.

Cook shrimp, covered with grill lid, over medium-hot coals (350° to 400°) 3 minutes on each side or until shrimp turn pink. Squeeze lemon over shrimp and serve. **Yield: 4 servings.**

PER SERVING: 191 CALORIES (11% FROM FAT)
FAT 2.3G (SATURATED FAT 0.5G)
PROTEIN 35.9G CARBOHYDRATE 4.2G
CHOLESTEROL 332MG SODIUM 385MG

Meatless Main Dishes

Enjoy our best bean, pasta, and cheese entrées.
These dishes prove that eating meatless meals doesn't mean
settling for less taste or less nutrition.

Black Bean-and-Barley Salad, Mamma Mia Pasta, Artichoke Quiche

Mediterranean Ravioli, Roasted Chiles Rellenos with Tomatillo Sauce, Fiesta Quiche

Vegetable-Cheese Enchiladas, Fettuccine Primavera, Light Chiles Rellenos

Lentil Spaghetti Sauce, Three-Bean Enchiladas, Vegetable Burritos

Vegetable Pizzas (page 70)

Black Bean-and-Barley Salad

Black Bean-and-Barley Salad

¾ cup barley, uncooked
¼ cup lime juice
2 tablespoons water
1 tablespoon vegetable oil
1 teaspoon sugar
½ teaspoon garlic powder
¼ teaspoon salt
¼ teaspoon ground black pepper
¼ teaspoon ground cumin
¼ teaspoon ground red pepper
1 (15-ounce) can black beans, drained and
    rinsed
Leaf lettuce
1 cup chopped tomato
¼ cup (2 ounces) shredded reduced-fat
    Cheddar cheese
¼ cup sliced green onions

Cook barley according to package directions; drain and set aside.

Combine lime juice and next 8 ingredients in a jar. Cover tightly, and shake vigorously.

Pour half of dressing over barley; cover and chill 8 hours, stirring mixture occasionally.

Combine beans and remaining dressing; cover and chill 8 hours, stirring occasionally.

Spoon barley mixture evenly onto lettuce-lined plates. Top evenly with black beans, tomato, cheese, and green onions. **Yield: 4 servings**.

PER SERVING: 342 CALORIES (20% FROM FAT)
FAT 7.6G (SATURATED FAT 0.3G)
PROTEIN 17.4G CARBOHYDRATE 53.7G
CHOLESTEROL 10MG SODIUM 260MG

Black Bean Terrine with Fresh Tomato Coulis and Jalapeño Sauce

3 (15-ounce) cans black beans, drained and rinsed
⅓ cup egg substitute
1½ teaspoons salt-free, extra-spicy herb-and-spice blend
1½ teaspoons ground cumin
¼ teaspoon freshly ground pepper
Vegetable cooking spray
Fresh Tomato Coulis
Jalapeño Sauce

Position knife blade in food processor bowl; add first 5 ingredients, and process until smooth, stopping occasionally to scrape down sides.

Pack bean mixture into an 8½- x 4½- x 3-inch loafpan coated with cooking spray. Cover with aluminum foil, and place in a large, shallow pan. Add hot water to large pan to depth of 1 inch. Bake at 350° for 55 to 60 minutes or until a knife inserted in center comes out clean.

Remove loafpan from water, and place a small weight on top of bean mixture; cover and chill 8 hours. Cut into 16 (½-inch) slices; serve each slice with 1½ tablespoons Fresh Tomato Coulis and 1 tablespoon Jalapeño Sauce. **Yield: 16 slices.**

Note: For salt-free, extra-spicy herb-and-spice blend, we used extra-spicy Mrs. Dash.

Fresh Tomato Coulis

4 medium to large tomatoes, peeled and seeded
1 clove garlic, halved
3 tablespoons chopped fresh cilantro
2 tablespoons rice wine vinegar
1 teaspoon dried thyme
1 teaspoon freshly ground pepper

Place tomatoes in container of an electric blender; process until smooth. Set puree aside.

Place colander in a large bowl; line colander with 2 layers of cheesecloth or a coffee filter. Pour puree into colander; cover loosely with plastic wrap, and chill 24 hours. Discard liquid in bowl.

Combine puree, garlic, and remaining ingredients in container of an electric blender; process until smooth. **Yield: 1½ cups.**

Jalapeño Sauce

¾ cup plain nonfat yogurt
1 clove garlic, minced
¼ cup seeded and chopped jalapeño peppers
¼ cup chopped fresh cilantro
1 teaspoon frozen unsweetened orange juice concentrate, thawed
½ teaspoon ground cumin
¼ teaspoon salt

Combine all ingredients in a small bowl. **Yield: 1 cup.**

PER SERVING: 136 CALORIES (6% FROM FAT)
FAT 0.9G (SATURATED FAT 0.1G)
PROTEIN 9.3G CARBOHYDRATE 24.5G
CHOLESTEROL 0MG SODIUM 289MG

What are Legumes?

Legumes are plants that produce pods containing edible seeds.
• The best known legumes are black beans, black-eyed peas, chick-peas, kidney beans, lentils, split peas, pinto beans, and white beans.
• Legumes are loaded with complex carbohydrates, fiber, vitamins, minerals, and protein.
• For an added bonus, legumes have no cholesterol and are very low in fat and sodium.

Fettuccine Primavera

1 small onion, chopped
Vegetable cooking spray
1 (10-ounce) package frozen snow pea pods,
     thawed
1 sweet red pepper, cut into thin strips
1 cup fresh broccoli flowerets
½ cup sliced fresh mushrooms
Alfredo Sauce
1 (12-ounce) package fettuccine, cooked
     without salt or fat

Cook onion in a large nonstick skillet coated with cooking spray over medium heat, stirring constantly, until tender. Add snow peas and next 3 ingredients; cook, stirring constantly, until vegetables are crisp-tender.

Stir in Alfredo Sauce; add fettuccine, and toss gently. Serve immediately. **Yield: 6 servings.**

Alfredo Sauce

2 cups nonfat cottage cheese
3 tablespoons grated Parmesan cheese
2 tablespoons butter-flavored granules
½ cup evaporated skimmed milk
½ teaspoon chicken-flavored bouillon
     granules
½ teaspoon dried basil
¼ teaspoon ground black pepper
Dash of ground red pepper

Combine all ingredients in container of an electric blender; process until smooth, stopping once to scrape down sides.

Pour into a small saucepan; cook sauce over low heat, stirring constantly, until thoroughly heated. **Yield: 2¾ cups.**

PER SERVING: 339 CALORIES (6% FROM FAT)
FAT 2.1G (SATURATED FAT 0.7G)
PROTEIN 23.3G CARBOHYDRATE 57.1G
CHOLESTEROL 6MG SODIUM 509MG

Mamma Mia Pasta

6 ounces wheel-shaped (rotelle) pasta,
     uncooked
4 cloves garlic, minced
1 medium onion, finely chopped
2 teaspoons olive oil
1 (14½-ounce) can no-salt-added whole
     tomatoes, undrained and chopped
1 tablespoon tomato paste
2 teaspoons sugar
2 teaspoons dried oregano
1 teaspoon dried basil
¼ teaspoon salt
¼ teaspoon freshly ground pepper
¼ cup freshly grated Parmesan cheese
½ cup (2 ounces) shredded part-skim
     mozzarella cheese, divided

Cook pasta according to package directions, omitting salt and oil; drain pasta, and set aside.

Cook garlic and onion in olive oil in a large skillet over medium heat until tender. Add tomatoes and next 6 ingredients; cook 5 minutes.

Add Parmesan cheese and ¼ cup mozzarella cheese, stirring until cheese melts. Pour over cooked pasta. Sprinkle with remaining ¼ cup mozzarella cheese. **Yield: 3 servings.**

PER SERVING: 389 CALORIES (22% FROM FAT)
FAT 9.6G (SATURATED FAT 2.8G)
PROTEIN 17.4G CARBOHYDRATE 59.2G
CHOLESTEROL 16MG SODIUM 479MG

Pasta Fasta

Save time by cooking extra pasta for another meal. Toss it with a small amount of olive oil, and store in a covered container in the refrigerator up to 3 days.

To reheat, place pasta in a colander, and pour hot water over it.

Mediterranean Ravioli

Mediterranean Ravioli

Vegetable cooking spray
2 teaspoons olive oil
½ pound eggplant, peeled and cut into
   ½-inch cubes
1 cup chopped onion
2 cloves garlic, minced
1 (15-ounce) container refrigerated light
   chunky tomato sauce
2 tablespoons sliced ripe olives
1 tablespoon balsamic vinegar
1 teaspoon dried thyme
1 (9-ounce) package refrigerated, light
   cheese-filled ravioli, uncooked
3 tablespoons grated Parmesan cheese

Coat a large nonstick skillet with cooking
spray. Add olive oil; place over medium-high heat.
  Add eggplant, onion, and garlic; cook, stirring
constantly, 5 minutes or until tender. Stir in
tomato sauce and next 3 ingredients; remove
from heat.

Cook ravioli according to package directions;
drain. Rinse and drain. Toss with vegetables;
place in a 1½-quart shallow baking dish coated
with cooking spray. Sprinkle with cheese.
  Bake at 350° for 30 minutes. **Yield: 4 servings**.

PER SERVING: 288 CALORIES (25% FROM FAT)
FAT 7.9G (SATURATED FAT 2.6G)
PROTEIN 14.1G CARBOHYDRATE 40.0G
CHOLESTEROL 44MG SODIUM 771MG

Lentil Spaghetti Sauce

Vegetable cooking spray
¾ cup chopped onion
2 cloves garlic, minced
4 cups water
1½ cups dried lentils, uncooked
1 teaspoon crushed red pepper
¾ teaspoon salt
½ teaspoon pepper
1 (14½-ounce) can no-salt-added whole
   tomatoes, undrained and chopped
1 (6-ounce) can no-salt-added tomato paste
1 tablespoon white vinegar
2 beef-flavored bouillon cubes
½ teaspoon dried basil
½ teaspoon dried oregano
8 cups hot cooked spaghetti (cooked without
   salt or fat)

Coat a Dutch oven with cooking spray. Add
onion and garlic; cook until tender, stirring constantly. Add next 5 ingredients. Bring to a boil;
cover, reduce heat, and simmer 30 minutes.
  Add tomatoes and next 5 ingredients. Bring to a
boil; reduce heat, and simmer 45 minutes to 1 hour
or to desired thickness, stirring often. Serve over
hot cooked spaghetti. **Yield: 8 servings**.

PER SERVING: 357 CALORIES (4% FROM FAT)
FAT 1.6G (SATURATED FAT 0.2G)
PROTEIN 18.3G CARBOHYDRATE 68.6G
CHOLESTEROL 0MG SODIUM 347MG

Vegetable Pizzas

(pictured on page 65)

6 (8-inch) Skillet Pizza Crusts
1½ cups commercial reduced-fat pasta sauce
1 cup sliced fresh mushrooms
1 cup (4 ounces) shredded part-skim
      mozzarella cheese
¾ cup chopped green pepper
½ cup chopped onion
¼ cup sliced ripe olives

Place pizza crusts on baking sheets. Spread each crust with ¼ cup pasta sauce, and sprinkle evenly with remaining ingredients.

Bake at 425° for 12 to 15 minutes or until edges are lightly browned and cheese melts. Cut into wedges. **Yield: 6 servings.**

Skillet Pizza Crusts

3 packages active dry yeast
1 teaspoon sugar
¾ cup warm water (105° to 115°)
3 cups all-purpose flour
1 teaspoon salt
½ cup warm water (105° to 115°)
2 tablespoons olive oil
Vegetable cooking spray

Combine first 3 ingredients in a 2-cup liquid measuring cup; let stand 5 minutes.

Combine yeast mixture, flour, and next 3 ingredients in a large bowl, stirring until well blended.

Turn dough out onto a lightly floured surface, and knead 5 minutes. Place in a bowl coated with cooking spray, turning to grease top.

Cover and let rise in a warm place (85°), free from drafts, 30 minutes or until doubled in bulk.

Punch dough down, and knead lightly 4 or 5 times. Divide dough into 6 equal portions; roll each into an 8-inch circle.

Cook each round on one side in an 8-inch

nonstick skillet coated with cooking spray over medium heat about 2 minutes or until lightly browned. **Yield: 6 (8-inch) pizza crusts.**

Note: Cooled crusts may be frozen in an airtight container up to 6 months.

PER SERVING: 391 CALORIES (24% FROM FAT)
FAT 10.3G (SATURATED FAT 2.8G)
PROTEIN 14.3G CARBOHYDRATE 59.9G
CHOLESTEROL 11MG SODIUM 607MG

Artichoke Quiche

2 cups cooked rice (cooked without salt or fat)
¾ cup (3 ounces) shredded farmer cheese,
      divided
¾ cup egg substitute, divided
1 teaspoon dried dill
Vegetable cooking spray
1 (14-ounce) can artichoke hearts, drained
      and quartered
¾ cup skim milk
¼ cup thinly sliced green onions
2 teaspoons Dijon mustard
¼ teaspoon ground white pepper

Combine rice, ¼ cup cheese, ¼ cup egg substitute, and dill; press mixture into a 9-inch pieplate coated with cooking spray. Bake at 350° for 5 minutes.

Arrange artichokes in rice crust; sprinkle with remaining ½ cup cheese. Combine remaining ½ cup egg substitute, skim milk, and remaining ingredients; pour over cheese.

Bake at 350° for 50 minutes or until set. Let stand 5 minutes; serve warm. **Yield: 6 servings.**

PER SERVING: 163 CALORIES (18% FROM FAT)
FAT 3.5G (SATURATED FAT 0.1G)
PROTEIN 11.3G CARBOHYDRATE 23.8G
CHOLESTEROL 1MG SODIUM 163MG

Artichoke Quiche

Fiesta Quiche

Fiesta Quiche

Vegetable cooking spray
4 (8½-inch) flour tortillas
½ cup (2 ounces) shredded reduced-fat
    Cheddar cheese
1 (4.5-ounce) can chopped green chiles,
    drained
¼ cup sliced green onions
½ cup picante sauce
1 cup egg substitute
⅓ cup skim milk
½ teaspoon chili powder
¼ teaspoon cracked black pepper
6 tomato slices
2 tablespoons plain nonfat yogurt
Fresh cilantro

Coat a 12-inch quiche dish with cooking spray; layer tortillas in dish. Sprinkle cheese, chiles, and green onions over tortillas; dollop with picante sauce.

Combine egg substitute and next 3 ingredients; pour into quiche dish.

Bake at 350° for 30 to 35 minutes. Remove from oven, and arrange tomato slices around edge of quiche; top each tomato slice with 1 teaspoon yogurt and a sprig of cilantro. Cut into wedges. **Yield: 6 servings.**

PER SERVING: 238 CALORIES (22% FROM FAT)
FAT 5.7G (SATURATED FAT 1.7G)
PROTEIN 12.6G CARBOHYDRATE 33.7G
CHOLESTEROL 6MG SODIUM 675MG

Three-Bean Enchiladas

½ cup dried kidney beans
½ cup dried navy beans
½ cup dried pinto beans
6 cups water
½ teaspoon salt
½ cup chopped onion
2 cloves garlic
1 teaspoon chili powder
1 teaspoon ground cumin
¼ teaspoon salt
1 (4.5-ounce) can chopped green chiles,
    undrained
12 (6-inch) corn tortillas
Vegetable cooking spray
1 (10-ounce) can enchilada sauce
1 cup (4 ounces) shredded 40%-less-fat
    Monterey Jack cheese

Sort and wash beans; place in a Dutch oven. Cover with water 2 inches above beans, and bring to a boil; cover and cook 2 minutes. Remove from heat, and let stand 1 hour. Drain beans; return to Dutch oven.

Add 6 cups water and ½ teaspoon salt to beans. Bring to a boil; cover, reduce heat, and simmer 1 hour or until beans are tender. Drain, reserving ¼ cup liquid (add water, if necessary, to make ¼ cup).

Place beans in container of an electric blender; add reserved ¼ cup liquid, onion, and next 5 ingredients. Process 5 seconds or until chunky.

Brush tortillas with water. Divide bean mixture among tortillas. Roll up; place, seam side down, in a 13- x 9- x 2-inch baking dish coated with cooking spray. Top with enchilada sauce.

Cover and bake at 350° for 20 minutes. Top with cheese, and bake, uncovered, 5 minutes.
Yield: 6 servings.

PER SERVING: 373 CALORIES (16% FROM FAT)
FAT 6.6G (SATURATED FAT 2.4G)
PROTEIN 20.5G CARBOHYDRATE 61.1G
CHOLESTEROL 12MG SODIUM 700MG

Vegetable-Cheese Enchiladas

8 (6-inch) corn tortillas
1 medium zucchini, cut into ½-inch cubes
1 cup (4 ounces) shredded reduced-fat
    Monterey Jack cheese, divided
1 cup cooked brown rice (cooked without salt
    or fat)
¼ cup chopped green onions
⅓ cup low-fat sour cream
¼ teaspoon salt
¼ teaspoon pepper
Vegetable cooking spray
2 (10-ounce) cans chopped tomatoes and
    green chiles, undrained

Wrap tortillas in aluminum foil, and bake at 350° for 7 minutes.

Cook zucchini in boiling water to cover 2 minutes; drain and pat dry with paper towels.

Combine zucchini, half of cheese, and next 5 ingredients. Spoon mixture evenly down center of each tortilla; fold opposite sides over filling, and roll up tortillas. Place, seam side down, in an 11- x 7- x 1½-inch baking dish coated with cooking spray.

Pour chopped tomatoes and green chiles over tortillas.

Bake at 350° for 15 minutes; sprinkle with remaining cheese, and bake 5 additional minutes.
Yield: 4 servings.

PER SERVING: 343 CALORIES (26% FROM FAT)
FAT 9.9G (SATURATED FAT 4.9G)
PROTEIN 14.1G CARBOHYDRATE 47.3G
CHOLESTEROL 26MG SODIUM 1031MG

Vegetable Burritos

Vegetable Burritos

4½ cups sliced fresh mushrooms (1 pound)
1 cup chopped onion
1 cup chopped green pepper
2 cloves garlic, crushed
2 teaspoons olive oil
1 (15-ounce) can kidney beans, drained
2 tablespoons finely chopped ripe olives
¼ teaspoon pepper
8 (8-inch) flour tortillas
½ cup nonfat sour cream
1 cup commercial chunky salsa, divided
¾ cup (3 ounces) shredded, reduced-fat sharp
   Cheddar cheese
Vegetable cooking spray
Garnish: fresh cilantro

Cook first 4 ingredients in olive oil in a large, nonstick skillet over medium-high heat, stirring constantly, until tender. Remove from heat; drain. Combine cooked vegetables, kidney beans, olives, and pepper.

Spoon about ½ cup bean mixture evenly down center of each tortilla. Top with 1 tablespoon sour cream, 1 tablespoon salsa, and 1½ tablespoons cheese; fold opposite sides over filling.

Coat a large nonstick skillet or griddle with cooking spray. Place over medium-high heat until hot. Cook tortillas, seam side down, 1 minute on each side or until thoroughly heated. Top each tortilla with 1 tablespoon salsa. Garnish, if desired. **Yield: 8 servings.**

PER SERVING: 316 CALORIES (22% FROM FAT)
FAT 7.6G (SATURATED FAT 2.0G)
PROTEIN 15.0G CARBOHYDRATE 47.9G
CHOLESTEROL 7MG SODIUM 528MG

Light Chiles Rellenos

6 ounces ⅓-less-fat Monterey Jack cheese
3 (4.5-ounce) cans whole green chiles, drained
¼ cup egg substitute
⅛ teaspoon salt
⅛ teaspoon pepper
4 egg whites
Vegetable cooking spray
½ cup all-purpose flour
1 (14½-ounce) can no-salt-added stewed
   tomatoes, undrained and chopped

Cut cheese into 9 (2- x ½- x ½-inch) pieces; place 1 piece inside each chile. (Cheese pieces may need trimming slightly to fit chiles.) Set chiles aside.

Combine egg substitute, salt, and pepper in a large bowl. Beat egg whites until stiff peaks form; fold into egg substitute mixture.

Place a large nonstick skillet coated with cooking spray over medium heat. Quickly dredge cheese-filled chiles in flour, and coat each generously with egg white mixture. Place coated chiles in skillet, and brown on both sides.

Transfer browned chiles to a 13- x 9- x 2-inch baking dish coated with cooking spray. Pour tomatoes over chiles, and bake at 350° for 30 minutes. **Yield: 3 servings.**

PER SERVING: 384 CALORIES (30% FROM FAT)
FAT 13.0G (SATURATED FAT 7.0G)
PROTEIN 31.2G CARBOHYDRATE 36.5G
CHOLESTEROL 42MG SODIUM 653MG

Low-Fat Secrets

Here are tips for reducing the fat in traditional Chiles Rellenos.
• Substitute ⅓-less-fat Monterey Jack for regular cheese.
• Use an equivalent amount of egg substitute in place of an egg yolk.

Roasted Chiles Rellenos with Tomatillo Sauce

8 Anaheim chile peppers
10 tomatillos, husked
1 small onion, sliced
2 cloves garlic, minced
¼ teaspoon salt
¼ teaspoon pepper
¼ teaspoon ground cumin
2 tablespoons chopped fresh cilantro
¾ cup canned black beans, drained and
    rinsed
1 cup (4 ounces) shredded reduced-fat
    Monterey Jack cheese
1 egg white
¼ cup egg substitute
¾ cup all-purpose flour
1 teaspoon vegetable oil
Vegetable cooking spray

Place chile peppers, tomatillos, and onion on food rack of grill. Cook, covered with grill lid, over hot coals (400° to 500°) about 5 minutes on each side or until peppers look blistered, and tomatillos and onion are lightly browned.

Place peppers immediately in a heavy-duty, zip-top plastic bag; seal and chill at least 8 hours.

Place grilled vegetables in an airtight container; chill at least 8 hours.

Peel peppers, and remove seeds; set aside.

Combine tomatillos, onion, garlic, and next 3 ingredients in container of an electric blender. Process until smooth. Stir in cilantro; set tomatillo sauce aside.

Combine black beans and cheese; spoon into peppers (some peppers may split). Set aside.

Beat egg white at high speed of an electric mixer until stiff peaks form; gradually beat in egg substitute. Set aside.

Coat stuffed peppers with flour; dip in egg white mixture. Lightly recoat peppers with flour.

Add oil to a large nonstick skillet coated with cooking spray. Cook chiles in hot oil on both sides until lightly browned. Serve immediately with tomatillo sauce. **Yield: 4 servings.**

PER SERVING: 311 CALORIES (24% FROM FAT)
FAT 8.3G (SATURATED FAT 3.2G)
PROTEIN 18.9G CARBOHYDRATE 42.8G
CHOLESTEROL 19MG SODIUM 523MG

Low-Fat Ingredient Substitutions

Item	Substitution	Item	Substitution
DAIRY PRODUCTS		**FATS AND OILS**	
Cheeses	Cheeses with 5 grams of fat or less per ounce (American, Cheddar, colby, edam, Monterey Jack, mozzarella, Swiss)	Butter or Margarine	Reduced-calorie margarine or margarine with liquid polyunsaturated or monounsaturated oil listed as the first ingredient; also, polyunsaturated or monounsaturated oil
Cottage cheese	Nonfat or 1% low-fat cottage cheese		
Cream cheese	Nonfat or light process cream cheese, Neufchâtel cheese	Chocolate, unsweetened	3 tablespoons unsweetened cocoa plus 1 tablespoon polyunsaturated oil or margarine
Ricotta cheese	Nonfat, lite, or part-skim ricotta cheese	Mayonnaise	Nonfat or reduced-calorie mayonnaise
Ice cream	Nonfat or low-fat frozen yogurt, low-fat frozen dairy dessert, low-fat ice cream, sherbet, sorbet	Oil	Polyunsaturated or monounsaturated oil in reduced amount
Milk, whole or 2%	Skim milk, ½% milk, 1% milk, evaporated skimmed milk diluted equally with water	Salad dressing	Nonfat or oil-free salad dressing
Sour cream	Nonfat sour cream, light sour cream, low-fat or nonfat yogurt	Shortening	Polyunsaturated or monounsaturated oil in amount reduced by one-third
Whipping cream	Chilled evaporated skimmed milk, whipped		

Meats

With today's beef and pork being leaner than ever before, make these juicy meats part of your low-fat eating plan. Select entrées for any occasion—from casual suppers to elegant dinners.

American Steakhouse Beef, Mustard Marinated Sirloin, Lemon Veal

Stewed Lamb with Five Spices, Barbecued Pork Loin Roast, Chile-Beef Kabobs

Beef and Cauliflower over Rice, French-Style Beef Roast, Cornbread-Tamale Pie

Hopping John with Grilled Pork Medaillons, Country Sausage

Steak au Poivre (page 80)

French-Style Beef Roast

French-Style Beef Roast

1 (3-pound) boneless beef rump roast
1 large clove garlic, quartered
1 teaspoon dried thyme
½ teaspoon pepper
1 bay leaf
4 cups water
1 pound turnips, peeled and quartered
¾ pound onions, quartered
2 cups (2-inch pieces) carrot
1 cup (2-inch pieces) celery
Garnish: fresh parsley sprig

Trim all visible fat from roast. Place roast in a large Dutch oven; add garlic and next 4 ingredients. Bring to a boil. Cover, reduce heat, and simmer 2½ hours.

Add turnip, onion, carrot, and celery to roast. Cover and cook an additional 30 minutes or until vegetables are tender.

Remove roast to a serving platter; let roast stand 10 minutes before slicing. Arrange vegetables around roast. Strain broth, and serve with roast. Garnish, if desired. **Yield: 10 servings.**

PER SERVING: 187 CALORIES (23% FROM FAT)
FAT 4.7G (SATURATED FAT 1.7G)
PROTEIN 26.5G CARBOHYDRATE 8.7G
CHOLESTEROL 64MG SODIUM 104MG

Lean Meats

The recipes included here call for the leanest cuts of meats with little, if any, added fat.

Although most of our dishes derive 30 percent or less of their calories from fat, some cuts of meat are naturally higher in fat content.

Marinated Sauerbraten Beef

1 pound trimmed top round roast
Vegetable cooking spray
2 cups water
1 cup Burgundy or other dry red wine
2 small onions, thinly sliced
2 tablespoons pickling spice
2 tablespoons brown sugar
1 teaspoon salt
10 black peppercorns, crushed
2 bay leaves
Sauerbraten Sauce

Brown roast in a Dutch oven coated with cooking spray. Combine water and next 7 ingredients; reserve 1 cup mixture for Sauerbraten Sauce. Pour remaining mixture over roast. Cover; chill 8 hours.

Remove Dutch oven from refrigerator; uncover and place over medium heat. Bring to a boil; cover, reduce heat, and simmer 45 minutes or until tender. Drain. Remove and discard bay leaves. Slice roast, and serve with Sauerbraten Sauce. **Yield: 3 servings.**

Sauerbraten Sauce

1 cup reserved marinade
¼ cup gingersnap crumbs
¼ cup nonfat sour cream

Combine first 2 ingredients in a heavy saucepan; cook over medium heat, stirring constantly, until thickened. Reduce heat; stir in sour cream, and cook over low heat until thoroughly heated. (Do not boil.) **Yield: 1 cup.**

PER SERVING: 319 CALORIES (24% FROM FAT)
FAT 8.6G (SATURATED FAT 2.6G)
PROTEIN 33.3G CARBOHYDRATE 19.3G
CHOLESTEROL 84MG SODIUM 563MG

Steak au Poivre

(pictured on page 77)

6 (4-ounce) beef tenderloin steaks
1 clove garlic, crushed
1 teaspoon crushed black peppercorns
Vegetable cooking spray
⅓ cup chopped onion
1 cup green pepper strips
1 cup sweet red pepper strips
1 cup sweet yellow pepper strips
1 clove garlic, minced
½ teaspoon beef-flavored bouillon granules
½ teaspoon paprika
½ teaspoon crushed black peppercorns
½ cup water
½ cup evaporated skimmed milk
3 tablespoons brandy

Trim fat from steaks. Combine crushed garlic and 1 teaspoon peppercorns; press mixture into each side of steaks. Coat a nonstick skillet with cooking spray; place over medium heat until hot.

Arrange steaks in skillet, and cook to desired degree of doneness, turning once. Remove steaks to a serving platter, and keep steaks warm.

Wipe skillet with paper towels; coat with cooking spray, and place over medium heat until hot. Add onion and next 4 ingredients; cook, stirring constantly, until vegetables are crisp-tender. Spoon pepper mixture over steaks, and keep warm.

Combine bouillon granules and next 4 ingredients in a small bowl; stir well. Pour into skillet, and cook over medium heat, stirring often, until mixture is reduced to ⅔ cup.

Place brandy in a long-handled saucepan; heat until warm. Remove from heat. Ignite with a long match; pour into sauce mixture; stir until flames die down. Spoon over each steak. **Yield: 6 servings.**

PER SERVING: 182 CALORIES (35% FROM FAT)
FAT 7.0G (SATURATED FAT 2.7G)
PROTEIN 22.2G CARBOHYDRATE 6.7G
CHOLESTEROL 60MG SODIUM 150MG

Mustard Marinated Sirloin

2 tablespoons Dijon mustard
2 tablespoons Burgundy or other dry red wine
1 teaspoon coarsely ground pepper
2 cloves garlic, minced
1 pound lean, boneless sirloin steak, trimmed
Vegetable cooking spray
1 cup sliced fresh mushrooms
1½ tablespoons all-purpose flour
1 cup reduced-sodium, fat-free beef broth
½ cup Burgundy or other dry red wine
¼ teaspoon salt
¼ teaspoon pepper

Combine first 4 ingredients. Coat steak on both sides with mustard mixture, and place in a shallow dish. Cover and chill 8 hours.

Place steak on a rack coated with cooking spray; place rack in a broiler pan. Broil 3 inches from heat (with electric oven door partially opened) 4 to 5 minutes on each side or until desired degree of doneness. Let stand 5 minutes. Thinly slice steak diagonally across grain; keep steak warm.

Coat a nonstick skillet with cooking spray; add mushrooms, and cook, stirring constantly, over medium heat until tender.

Add flour; cook 1 minute, stirring constantly. Gradually add beef broth and ½ cup Burgundy; cook, stirring constantly, until thickened. Stir in salt and pepper. Spoon sauce evenly over meat. **Yield: 4 servings.**

PER SERVING: 213 CALORIES (29% FROM FAT)
FAT 6.8G (SATURATED FAT 2.4G)
PROTEIN 28.2G CARBOHYDRATE 6.5G
CHOLESTEROL 80MG SODIUM 435MG

Mustard Marinated Sirloin

American Steakhouse Beef

1 (1½-pound) trimmed lean boneless top
   sirloin steak
⅓ cup low-sodium soy sauce
⅓ cup unsweetened pineapple juice
⅓ cup dry sherry
¼ cup cider vinegar

Place steak in a large, shallow dish. Combine soy sauce and remaining ingredients; pour over steak. Cover and chill 4 hours, turning steak occasionally. Drain, discarding marinade.

Cook over hot coals (400° to 500°) 10 to 15 minutes on each side or to desired degree of doneness. To serve, slice across grain into thin slices. **Yield: 7 servings.**

PER SERVING: 210 CALORIES (33% FROM FAT)
FAT 7.8G (SATURATED FAT 3.2G)
PROTEIN 27.4G CARBOHYDRATE 0.3G
CHOLESTEROL 80MG SODIUM 96MG

Steak Kabobs

1½ pounds sirloin tip, trimmed
¼ cup low-sodium soy sauce
2 tablespoons brown sugar
½ teaspoon ground ginger
2 teaspoons dry sherry
1½ teaspoons vegetable oil
1 (15¼-ounce) can unsweetened pineapple
   chunks
4½ cups hot cooked rice (cooked without salt
   or fat)

Cut meat into ½-inch cubes; place in a shallow dish or a heavy-duty, zip-top plastic bag, and set aside.

Combine soy sauce and next 4 ingredients; pour over meat and cover or seal. Chill at least 3 hours. Drain meat, discarding marinade.

Drain pineapple, reserving juice for another use. Alternate meat and pineapple on 14-inch skewers.

Cook over medium-hot coals (350° to 400°) 8 minutes or until desired degree of doneness, turning often. Serve with rice. **Yield: 6 servings.**

PER SERVING: 382 CALORIES (18% FROM FAT)
FAT 7.5G (SATURATED FAT 2.7G)
PROTEIN 30.8G CARBOHYDRATE 45.2G
CHOLESTEROL 81MG SODIUM 191MG

Chile-Beef Kabobs

16 (1½-inch) onions
1 pound lean boneless sirloin, cut into
   16 pieces
16 medium-size fresh mushrooms
2 sweet red peppers, each cut into 8 pieces
2 sweet yellow peppers, each cut into 8 pieces
1 cup Red Chile Sauce, divided
½ cup Burgundy or other dry red wine
1 cup nonfat sour cream
Garnishes: jalapeño peppers, kale leaves

Cook onions in boiling water to cover 8 minutes; drain.

Alternate meat, onions, mushrooms, and peppers on 8 (14-inch) skewers; place skewers in a shallow dish.

Combine ½ cup Red Chile Sauce and wine. Pour over kabobs, turning to coat. Cover and chill 4 hours.

Remove kabobs from marinade, discarding marinade. Place kabobs on a rack; place rack in broiler pan.

Broil 5½ inches from heat (with electric oven door partially opened) 8 to 10 minutes, turning occasionally.

Combine sour cream and remaining ½ cup Red Chile Sauce. Serve with kabobs. Garnish, if desired. **Yield: 4 servings.**

Chile-Beef Kabobs

Red Chile Sauce

4 ounces dried Anaheim chile peppers
2 cloves garlic, minced
1 tablespoon vegetable oil
2 tablespoons all-purpose flour
2 cups water
1½ teaspoons ground cumin
¾ teaspoon salt

Remove pepper stems and seeds. (Wear rubber gloves when handling peppers.) Cover peppers with boiling water; let stand 30 minutes. Drain, reserving 1 cup liquid.

Position knife blade in food processor bowl; add peppers and reserved liquid. Process until smooth, stopping twice to scrape down sides. Set pepper mixture aside.

Cook garlic in oil in a heavy saucepan until

tender. Gradually stir in flour, and cook over medium heat, stirring constantly, until mixture is the color of caramel. Gradually add 2 cups water, stirring constantly. Stir in pepper mixture, and cook until slightly thickened.

Pour mixture through a wire-mesh strainer into a bowl, discarding solids remaining in strainer. Return to saucepan; add cumin and salt, and cook over medium heat until thickened. Sauce may be refrigerated up to 3 days or frozen up to 3 months. **Yield: 2¾ cups.**

Note: The Red Chile Sauce and sour cream mixture makes a spicy dip for raw vegetables or baked tortilla chips.

PER SERVING: 372 CALORIES (22% FROM FAT)
FAT 8.5G (SATURATED FAT 2.6G)
PROTEIN 36.8G CARBOHYDRATE 32.6G
CHOLESTEROL 80MG SODIUM 244MG

Beef and Cauliflower over Rice

1 pound boneless top round steak
3 tablespoons reduced-sodium soy sauce
Vegetable cooking spray
3 cups cauliflower flowerets
¾ cup coarsely chopped sweet red pepper
2 cloves garlic, minced
1 tablespoon cornstarch
¼ teaspoon beef-flavored bouillon granules
½ to 1 teaspoon dried crushed red pepper
½ teaspoon sugar
1 cup water
1 cup sliced green onions
2 cups hot cooked rice

Trim fat from steak; slice diagonally across grain into thin strips; place in a shallow dish. Coat with soy sauce; cover. Chill 30 minutes.

Coat a Dutch oven with cooking spray; place over medium heat until hot. Add meat and cook, stirring until browned. Reduce heat; cover and cook 10 minutes. Stir in cauliflower, sweet red pepper, and garlic; cover and cook 5 minutes.

Combine cornstarch and next 4 ingredients, stirring until smooth; stir into meat. Add green onions; bring to a boil. Cook, stirring constantly, 1 minute. Serve over rice. **Yield: 4 servings.**

PER SERVING: 305 CALORIES (14% FROM FAT)
FAT 4.9G (SATURATED FAT 1.8G)
PROTEIN 29.1G CARBOHYDRATE 35.1G
CHOLESTEROL 61MG SODIUM 506MG

Beef Hash

1 cup cubed cooked lean beef
1 cup peeled, cubed potato
½ cup chopped onion
1 tablespoon chopped fresh parsley
¼ teaspoon salt
¼ teaspoon pepper
2 teaspoons vegetable oil
⅓ cup skim milk

Combine first 6 ingredients; cook in hot oil in a large nonstick skillet over medium-high heat, stirring occasionally, 10 minutes or until mixture is browned and tender. Stir in milk; cover, reduce heat, and simmer 5 minutes. **Yield: 2 servings.**

PER SERVING: 282 CALORIES (30% FROM FAT)
FAT 9.4G (SATURATED FAT 1.7G)
PROTEIN 26.9G CARBOHYDRATE 21.5G
CHOLESTEROL 63MG SODIUM 366MG

Deli-Style Roast Beef

1 (4-pound) eye round roast, trimmed
5 cloves garlic, halved
1 (8-ounce) can tomato sauce
1 cup Burgundy or other dry red wine
¼ cup Worcestershire sauce
¼ cup lemon juice
¼ cup Creole mustard
2 tablespoons hot sauce
2 tablespoons prepared horseradish
2 teaspoons onion powder
2 bay leaves
Vegetable cooking spray

Cut 10 slits in roast; insert garlic halves into slits. Place in a heavy-duty, zip-top plastic bag.

Combine tomato sauce and next 8 ingredients; reserve ⅓ cup marinade. Pour remaining marinade over roast; seal bag. Chill 8 hours.

Remove roast from marinade, discarding marinade. Place on a rack in a roasting pan coated with cooking spray; insert meat thermometer.

Bake at 325° for 1 hour and 30 minutes or until thermometer registers 145° (medium-rare), basting 3 times with ⅓ cup reserved marinade. Remove from oven; wrap roast securely in plastic wrap to retain moisture. Chill roast several hours before slicing. **Yield: 15 servings.**

PER SERVING: 171 CALORIES (29% FROM FAT)
FAT 5.6G (SATURATED FAT 2.1G)
PROTEIN 24.5G CARBOHYDRATE 1.9G
CHOLESTEROL 57MG SODIUM 169MG

Cornbread-Tamale Pie

Vegetable cooking spray
1 pound ground round
1 cup chopped onion
1 cup chopped green pepper
1 clove garlic, minced
2 (8-ounce) cans no-salt-added tomato sauce
1 (12-ounce) can no-salt-added whole kernel corn, drained
10 ripe olives, sliced
1 tablespoon sugar
1 tablespoon chili powder
⅛ teaspoon salt
¼ teaspoon pepper
¾ cup (3 ounces) shredded, reduced-fat sharp Cheddar cheese
¾ cup yellow cornmeal
½ teaspoon salt
2 cups water
1 tablespoon reduced-calorie margarine

Coat a large, nonstick skillet with cooking spray; place over medium heat. Add ground round; cook until browned, stirring until it crumbles. Drain and pat dry with paper towels. Wipe pan drippings from skillet with a paper towel.

Coat skillet with cooking spray. Add onion, green pepper, and garlic; cook until vegetables are tender.

Stir in ground round, tomato sauce, and next 6 ingredients. Simmer, uncovered, 15 to 20 minutes.

Add Cheddar cheese, stirring until cheese melts. Spoon into an 8-inch square baking dish coated with cooking spray.

Combine cornmeal, ½ teaspoon salt, and water in a saucepan; bring to a boil, stirring constantly. Reduce heat, and cook, stirring constantly, until mixture thickens (about 3 minutes). Stir in margarine.

Spoon over meat mixture to within 1 inch of edge. Bake at 375° for 40 minutes or until topping is golden. **Yield: 6 servings.**

Note: Freeze pie before topping with cornmeal mixture. Thaw in refrigerator 24 hours. Remove from refrigerator, and let stand at room temperature 30 minutes; proceed as directed, baking 45 to 50 minutes.

PER SERVING: 325 CALORIES (29% FROM FAT)
FAT 10.4G (SATURATED FAT 3.6G)
PROTEIN 24.1G CARBOHYDRATE 33.7G
CHOLESTEROL 56MG SODIUM 491MG

Lemon Veal

1 tablespoon all-purpose flour
1 teaspoon beef-flavored bouillon granules
½ teaspoon paprika
½ teaspoon chopped fresh parsley
¼ teaspoon dried rosemary
⅛ teaspoon pepper
½ pound boneless round rump veal, trimmed and cut into 1-inch cubes
Vegetable cooking spray
2 medium carrots, scraped and cut into thin strips
¼ cup dry white wine
¼ cup water
1 tablespoon lemon juice
2 cups hot cooked rice (cooked without salt or fat)

Combine first 6 ingredients in a heavy-duty, zip-top plastic bag; add veal, seal bag, and shake to coat.

Coat a nonstick skillet with cooking spray; place over medium heat until hot. Add veal, and cook, stirring constantly, until lightly browned.

Add carrot and next 3 ingredients; bring to a boil, stirring constantly. Cover, reduce heat, and simmer 40 minutes. Serve over rice. **Yield: 2 servings.**

PER SERVING: 472 CALORIES (14% FROM FAT)
FAT 7.3G (SATURATED FAT 1.8G)
PROTEIN 32.5G CARBOHYDRATE 61.3G
CHOLESTEROL 100MG SODIUM 577MG

Stewed Lamb with Five Spices

Stewed Lamb with Five Spices

1 (3½-pound) leg of lamb
Vegetable cooking spray
2 **cups chopped onion**
4 **cloves garlic, minced**
1 **teaspoon ground coriander**
¼ **teaspoon salt**
½ **teaspoon paprika**
½ **teaspoon ground cumin**
½ **teaspoon ground ginger**
⅛ **teaspoon ground turmeric**
1 **(16-ounce) can no-salt-added tomatoes,
    undrained and chopped**
1 **lemon, sliced into wedges**
12 **pimiento-stuffed olives, sliced**
½ **cup chopped fresh parsley**
3 **cups hot cooked rice (cooked without salt
    or fat)**

Trim fat from lamb; bone and cut lamb into bite-size pieces. Set aside 1½ pounds of lamb; reserve remainder for another use.

Coat a nonstick skillet with cooking spray; place over medium-high heat until hot. Add lamb; cook until browned. Drain well.

Return lamb to skillet; add onion and garlic, and cook until onion is transparent. Stir in coriander and next 6 ingredients.

Transfer lamb mixture to a 3-quart baking dish; cover and bake at 375° for 1 to 1½ hours or until lamb is tender. Squeeze juice of lemon wedges into casserole; stir in lemon wedges, olives, and parsley.

Return to oven, and cook 5 minutes or until thoroughly heated. Serve over rice. **Yield: 6 servings.**

Per Serving: 310 Calories (19% from Fat)
Fat 6.4g (Saturated Fat 1.9g)
Protein 27.1g Carbohydrate 35.2g
Cholesterol 73mg Sodium 763mg

Barbecued Pork Loin Roast

1 (2¼-pound) boneless pork loin roast,
   trimmed
¾ cup no-salt-added ketchup
¾ cup finely chopped onion
1 tablespoon honey
1½ teaspoons unsweetened cocoa
1½ teaspoons brown sugar
2¼ teaspoons lemon juice
1½ teaspoons liquid smoke
⅛ teaspoon pepper
1 clove garlic, minced
Dash of mace
Vegetable cooking spray

Butterfly roast by making a lengthwise cut down center of one flat side, cutting to within ½ inch of other side. From bottom of cut, slice horizontally to within ½ inch from left side; repeat procedure to right side. Open roast. Place in a shallow dish; set aside.

Combine ketchup and next 9 ingredients; spread half of marinade mixture on roast, reserving remaining marinade.

Cover roast, and chill 8 hours. Cover and chill reserved marinade.

Remove roast from marinade, discarding marinade. Coat a grill rack with cooking spray; place rack on grill, and place roast on rack. Cook over medium-hot coals (350° to 400°) 10 minutes on each side or until meat thermometer inserted in thickest portion registers 160°. Remove roast from grill, and wrap in heavy-duty plastic wrap.

Cook reserved marinade in a heavy saucepan over medium-low heat 15 minutes, stirring often. Cut meat into thin slices, and serve with sauce. **Yield: 9 servings.**

PER SERVING: 178 CALORIES (21% FROM FAT)
FAT 4.2G (SATURATED FAT 1.4G)
PROTEIN 24.8G CARBOHYDRATE 9.4G
CHOLESTEROL 79MG SODIUM 66MG

Grilled Pork Tenderloin with Brown Sauce

8 cloves garlic, crushed
½ teaspoon pepper
¼ cup lime juice
1 tablespoon minced fresh oregano or
   1 teaspoon dried oregano
2 (¾-pound) pork tenderloins
Brown Sauce

Combine first 4 ingredients; set aside.

Trim excess fat from tenderloins, and place pork in a large, shallow dish. Spread lime mixture over tenderloins; cover and chill 3 hours, turning occasionally.

Remove tenderloins from marinade, reserving marinade. Boil marinade in a small saucepan 1 minute. Cook meat, covered with grill lid, over medium-hot coals (350° to 400°) 30 minutes, turning occasionally and basting with reserved marinade. Meat is done when meat thermometer inserted in thickest part of tenderloin registers 160°. Serve tenderloins with Brown Sauce. **Yield: 6 servings.**

Brown Sauce

2 tablespoons cornstarch
¾ teaspoon ground ginger
1½ cups canned low-sodium chicken broth
1½ tablespoons dry sherry
1½ tablespoons low-sodium soy sauce
½ teaspoon browning-and-seasoning sauce

Combine all ingredients in a heavy saucepan. Bring to a boil over medium heat; boil 1 minute, stirring constantly. **Yield: 1½ cups.**

PER SERVING: 181 CALORIES (24% FROM FAT)
FAT 4.8G (SATURATED FAT 1.6G)
PROTEIN 26.7G CARBOHYDRATE 6.1G
CHOLESTEROL 83MG SODIUM 179MG

Hopping John with Grilled Pork Medaillons

Hopping John with Grilled Pork Medaillons

¾ cup chopped onion
½ cup chopped celery
1 teaspoon olive oil
2 (16-ounce) cans ready-to-serve, no-salt-added, fat-free chicken broth
1 teaspoon dried thyme
½ cup wild rice, uncooked
1 cup frozen black-eyed peas
½ cup long-grain rice, uncooked
¾ cup chopped tomato
2 teaspoons lemon juice
2 tablespoons chopped fresh parsley
½ teaspoon salt
¼ teaspoon ground red pepper
¼ teaspoon freshly ground black pepper
Grilled Pork Medaillons
1 Red Delicious apple, cut into 12 wedges
Garnish: fresh thyme sprig

Cook onion and celery in olive oil in a large saucepan over medium heat, stirring constantly, until tender. Add chicken broth and dried thyme; bring mixture to a boil. Add wild rice. Cover, reduce heat, and cook 30 minutes.

Add black-eyed peas and next 7 ingredients; cover and cook 20 minutes or until rice is tender.

Serve with medaillons and apple wedges. Garnish, if desired. **Yield: 4 (1¼-cup) servings.**

Grilled Pork Medaillons

¼ cup lemon juice
2 tablespoons reduced-sodium soy sauce
2 cloves garlic, pressed
1 (¾-pound) pork tenderloin, trimmed
Vegetable cooking spray

Combine first 3 ingredients in a shallow container or a large heavy-duty, zip-top plastic bag. Add tenderloin; cover or seal and chill 8 hours.

Remove tenderloin from marinade, discarding marinade. Coat food rack with cooking spray; place rack on grill, and place tenderloin on rack.

Cook, covered with grill lid, over medium-hot coals (350° to 400°), 12 minutes on each side or until a meat thermometer registers 160°. Cut into 12 slices. **Yield: 4 servings.**

PER SERVING: 410 CALORIES (12% FROM FAT)
FAT 5.4G (SATURATED FAT 1.5G)
PROTEIN 29.7G CARBOHYDRATE 58.6G
CHOLESTEROL 63MG SODIUM 609MG

Fruit-Topped Pork Chops

1 tablespoon reduced-calorie margarine
¼ cup chopped celery
2 tablespoons chopped onion
1 cup herb-seasoned stuffing mix
3 (0.9-ounce) packages mixed dried fruit
2 tablespoons raisins
6 (4-ounce) lean, boneless center-cut loin pork chops (¾ inch thick)
¼ teaspoon salt
¼ teaspoon pepper
¼ cup all-purpose flour
Vegetable cooking spray
½ cup Chablis or other dry white wine

Melt margarine in a large skillet; add celery and onion. Cook, stirring constantly, until tender. Add stuffing mix, dried fruit, and raisins; toss.

Sprinkle pork chops with salt and pepper; dredge in flour. Coat a large nonstick skillet with cooking spray; add chops, and brown on both sides over medium heat.

Arrange chops in an 11- x 7- x 1½-inch baking dish coated with cooking spray; top with fruit mixture. Add wine to dish. Cover; bake at 350° for 40 to 45 minutes. **Yield: 3 servings.**

PER SERVING: 302 CALORIES (27% FROM FAT)
FAT 9.1G (SATURATED FAT 2.8G)
PROTEIN 28.2G CARBOHYDRATE 26.0G
CHOLESTEROL 80MG SODIUM 346MG

Creole-Style Pork Chops

4 (4-ounce) lean, boneless top loin pork chops
Vegetable cooking spray
½ cup chopped onion
½ cup chopped celery
½ cup chopped green pepper
½ cup chopped sweet red pepper
3 large cloves garlic, crushed
1 cup whole tomatoes, undrained and
    chopped
½ teaspoon hot sauce
¼ teaspoon pepper
2 cups hot cooked rice (cooked without salt
    or fat)
1 teaspoon cornstarch
¼ cup ready-to-serve, no-salt-added chicken
    broth

Trim fat from chops. Coat a nonstick skillet with cooking spray; place over medium-high heat until hot. Add pork chops, and brown on all sides. Remove from skillet.

Coat a nonstick skillet with cooking spray; place over medium-high heat until hot. Add onion and next 4 ingredients; cook until tender, stirring constantly. Remove ½ cup vegetable mixture from skillet; set aside.

Add tomato, hot sauce, and pepper to skillet. Return pork chops to skillet; cover and cook 15 minutes, turning pork chops once.

Stir reserved ½ cup vegetable mixture into rice; spoon onto a serving plate. Arrange pork chops on top of rice.

Combine cornstarch and chicken broth; add to vegetable mixture in skillet. Cook over medium heat, stirring constantly, until mixture begins to boil; boil 1 minute, stirring constantly, until thickened. Spoon over chops. **Yield: 4 servings.**

PER SERVING: 307 CALORIES (24% FROM FAT)
FAT 8.1G (SATURATED FAT 2.6G)
PROTEIN 24.0G CARBOHYDRATE 33.2G
CHOLESTEROL 60MG SODIUM 303MG

Black-Eyed Pea Jambalaya

1½ cups dried black-eyed peas
4 (10½-ounce) cans ready-to-serve, no-salt-
    added chicken broth
2 cups chopped tomato
1½ cups cubed lean cooked ham
1 cup chopped onion
¾ cup chopped green pepper
¼ cup chopped celery
2 cloves garlic, minced
1 bay leaf
½ teaspoon salt
¼ teaspoon dried thyme
⅛ teaspoon ground cloves
1½ cups long-grain rice, uncooked
1½ teaspoons hot sauce
½ cup sliced green onions

Sort and wash peas; place in a 5- or 6-quart pressure cooker. Add next 11 ingredients; stir well.

Close lid securely; according to manufacturer's directions, bring to high pressure over high heat (about 10 to 12 minutes). Reduce heat to medium-low or level needed to maintain high pressure; cook 15 minutes.

Remove from heat; run cold water over pressure cooker to reduce pressure instantly. Remove lid so that steam escapes away from you. Drain, reserving 3 cups liquid. Remove pea mixture from cooker, and keep warm. Discard bay leaf.

Add rice and reserved liquid to cooker. Close lid; bring to high pressure over high heat (about 5 minutes). Reduce heat to medium-low or level needed to maintain high pressure; cook 5 minutes.

Remove from heat; let stand 10 minutes or until pressure drops. Remove lid; add pea mixture, hot sauce, and green onions; toss. **Yield: 8 servings.**

PER SERVING: 228 CALORIES (8% FROM FAT)
FAT 2.0G (SATURATED FAT 0.6G)
PROTEIN 11.1G CARBOHYDRATE 40.2G
CHOLESTEROL 12MG SODIUM 538MG

Ham-and-Asparagus Fettuccine

1 pound fresh asparagus
2 cups chopped, reduced-fat, low-salt lean ham
Vegetable cooking spray
Alfredo Sauce
1 (12-ounce) package fettuccine, cooked
    without salt or fat

Snap off tough ends of asparagus. Remove scales from stalks with a knife or vegetable peeler, if desired. Cut diagonally into ½-inch slices.

Cook asparagus in a small amount of boiling water 3 minutes. Drain well, and set aside.

Cook ham over medium heat in a large nonstick skillet coated with cooking spray, stirring constantly, until thoroughly heated.

Stir in Alfredo Sauce; add fettuccine and asparagus, and toss gently before serving. **Yield: 6 servings.**

Alfredo Sauce

2 cups nonfat cottage cheese
3 tablespoons grated Parmesan cheese
2 tablespoons butter-flavored granules
½ cup evaporated skimmed milk
½ teaspoon chicken-flavored bouillon granules
½ teaspoon dried basil
¼ teaspoon ground black pepper
Dash of ground red pepper

Combine all ingredients in container of an electric blender; cover and process until smooth, stopping once to scrape down sides.

Pour into a small saucepan; cook sauce over low heat, stirring constantly, until thoroughly heated. **Yield: 2¾ cups.**

PER SERVING: 370 CALORIES (11% FROM FAT)
FAT 4.6G (SATURATED FAT 1.5G)
PROTEIN 30.4G CARBOHYDRATE 52.0G
CHOLESTEROL 33MG SODIUM 917MG

Ham-and-Asparagus Fettuccine

From left: Country Sausage, Chorizo, and Basic Meat Mixture

Basic Meat Mixture

4 pounds boneless, skinless turkey breast
2 pounds boneless pork loin
2 tablespoons browning-and-seasoning sauce
1 teaspoon salt

Position knife blade in food processor bowl; add half of turkey, pork, and seasonings. Process until smooth. Repeat procedure with remaining ingredients. **Yield: 6 pounds.**

PER POUND: 599 CALORIES (24% FROM FAT)
FAT 16.0G (SATURATED FAT 5.5G)
PROTEIN 102.4G CARBOHYDRATE 3.0G
CHOLESTEROL 272MG SODIUM 688MG

Country Sausage

1 pound Basic Meat Mixture
1 teaspoon rubbed sage
½ teaspoon black pepper
¼ teaspoon dried crushed red pepper
Vegetable cooking spray

Combine first 4 ingredients; shape into eight (2-ounce) patties. Coat a nonstick skillet with cooking spray; place over medium heat until hot.

Cook sausage patties 3 minutes on each side or until browned. **Yield: 4 servings.**

PER SERVING: 153 CALORIES (25% FROM FAT)
FAT 4.2G (SATURATED FAT 1.4G)
PROTEIN 25.7G CARBOHYDRATE 1.1G
CHOLESTEROL 68MG SODIUM 173MG

Chorizo

1 pound Basic Meat Mixture
¼ cup white vinegar
1 tablespoon dry sherry
2 teaspoons paprika
2 teaspoons chili powder
½ teaspoon dried oregano
½ teaspoon ground cumin
¼ teaspoon pepper
⅛ teaspoon ground cinnamon
⅛ teaspoon ground cloves
Pinch of ground coriander
Pinch of ground ginger
½ teaspoon browning-and-seasoning sauce
2 cloves garlic, crushed
1 yard sausage casing
½ cup water

Combine first 14 ingredients; divide into four (4-ounce) portions. Cut casing into four (8-inch) pieces; slip one end of each casing over sausage funnel tip. Force each portion through funnel into each casing; twist ends.

Bring water to a boil in a nonstick skillet; add sausage. Cover, reduce heat, and simmer 10 minutes. Uncover and cook over medium heat 5 minutes or until browned, turning occasionally.
Yield: 4 servings.

PER SERVING: 166 CALORIES (24% FROM FAT)
FAT 4.5G (SATURATED FAT 1.4G)
PROTEIN 26.1G CARBOHYDRATE 4.3G
CHOLESTEROL 68MG SODIUM 188MG

Poultry

Poultry is no longer reserved just for Sunday dinner. High in protein and low in fat and calories, poultry is a versatile, delicious, and smart choice any day of the week.

Lemon-Roasted Chicken, Old-Fashioned Chicken and Dumplings

Sherried Chicken with Artichokes, Grilled Lime Chicken with Black Bean Sauce

Poached Chicken Breast in Wine, Basil-Stuffed Chicken with Tomato-Basil Pasta

Tarragon Roasted Cornish Hens with Vegetables, Turkey Lasagna

Oven-Fried Chicken (page 94)

Lemon-Roasted Chicken

1½ teaspoons salt
2 teaspoons freshly ground pepper
2 to 3 teaspoons dried rosemary, crushed
1 (3-pound) broiler-fryer
1 medium lemon, cut in half

Combine first 3 ingredients; set aside.

Loosen skin from chicken breast by running fingers between the two; rub about 1 teaspoon seasoning mixture under skin. Rub remaining seasoning mixture over outside of chicken. Place chicken in a heavy-duty, zip-top plastic bag; seal and chill 8 hours.

Remove chicken from bag. Insert lemon halves in cavity; tie ends of legs together with string. Lift wing tips up and over back, and tuck under bird. Place chicken, breast side down, in a lightly greased shallow pan.

Bake at 450°, turning over every 15 minutes, for 50 minutes or until a meat thermometer registers 180°. Let chicken stand 10 minutes. Remove skin before serving. **Yield: 6 servings.**

PER SERVING: 172 CALORIES (35% FROM FAT)
FAT 6.6G (SATURATED FAT 1.8G)
PROTEIN 25.7G CARBOHYDRATE 1.0G
CHOLESTEROL 79MG SODIUM 662MG

Oven-Fried Chicken

(pictured on page 93)

½ cup crisp rice cereal crumbs
½ teaspoon pepper
½ teaspoon paprika
¼ teaspoon salt
4 (6-ounce) skinned chicken breast halves
Butter-flavored cooking spray

Combine first 4 ingredients in a shallow dish. Coat chicken with cooking spray; dredge in rice cereal mixture.

Place chicken on a baking sheet coated with cooking spray, and coat chicken again with cooking spray. Bake at 350° for 50 minutes or until done. **Yield: 4 servings.**

PER SERVING: 170 CALORIES (21% FROM FAT)
FAT 3.9G (SATURATED FAT 0.9G)
PROTEIN 28.3G CARBOHYDRATE 3.4G
CHOLESTEROL 77MG SODIUM 256MG

Poached Chicken Breast in Wine

4 (4-ounce) skinned and boned chicken breast halves
¾ cup Chablis or other dry white wine
2½ cups sliced fresh mushrooms
2 tablespoons chopped fresh parsley
½ teaspoon dried tarragon
½ teaspoon salt
¼ teaspoon pepper
1 tablespoon cornstarch
2 teaspoons water

Place chicken between two sheets of heavy-duty plastic wrap; flatten to ¼-inch thickness, using a meat mallet or rolling pin; set aside.

Combine Chablis and next 5 ingredients in a large skillet; bring to a boil over high heat. Arrange chicken in a single layer in skillet; cover, reduce heat, and simmer 15 minutes or until chicken is tender. Remove chicken to a platter; keep warm.

Combine cornstarch and water; stir into skillet. Bring mixture to a boil; boil 1 minute, stirring constantly. Pour sauce over chicken. **Yield: 4 servings.**

PER SERVING: 147 CALORIES (10% FROM FAT)
FAT 1.6G (SATURATED FAT 0.4G)
PROTEIN 27.3G CARBOHYDRATE 4.8G
CHOLESTEROL 66MG SODIUM 373MG

Dante's Chicken

Dante's Chicken

½ teaspoon ground ginger
½ teaspoon curry powder
⅛ teaspoon ground red pepper
4 (4-ounce) skinned and boned chicken breast
 halves
Vegetable cooking spray
2 cloves garlic, minced
3 tablespoons minced shallots
¼ cup sliced celery
½ cup sweet red pepper strips
½ cup canned chicken broth
½ cup Chablis or other dry white wine
¼ teaspoon ground ginger
Garnish: celery leaves

Combine first 3 ingredients; rub spice mixture on chicken. Set aside.

Coat a large nonstick skillet with cooking spray; place over medium-high heat until hot. Add garlic, shallots, celery, and red pepper strips; sauté 1 minute, stirring constantly. Remove from skillet.

Place chicken in skillet; cook until lightly browned, turning once. Return vegetables to skillet. Combine broth, Chablis, and ¼ teaspoon ginger; stir well. Pour over chicken. Cover, reduce heat, and simmer 15 minutes.

Arrange chicken and vegetables on a platter; garnish, if desired. **Yield: 4 servings.**

PER SERVING: 147 CALORIES (12% FROM FAT)
FAT 1.9G (SATURATED FAT 0.5G)
PROTEIN 27.4G CARBOHYDRATE 3.6G
CHOLESTEROL 66MG SODIUM 181MG

Chicken and Vegetables with Ginger-Soy Sauce

2 (4-ounce) skinned and boned chicken breast
   halves
¾ cup onion wedges
1 cup whole fresh mushrooms
¼ teaspoon onion powder
¼ teaspoon garlic powder
2 cups broccoli flowerets
1½ cups hot cooked rice (cooked without salt
   or fat)
Ginger-Soy Sauce

Layer chicken, onion, and mushrooms in a steamer basket over boiling water. Sprinkle with onion powder and garlic powder. Cover and steam 10 minutes.

Add broccoli; cover and steam 10 additional minutes or until chicken is tender.

Serve chicken and vegetables over rice; top with Ginger-Soy Sauce. **Yield: 2 servings.**

Ginger-Soy Sauce

1 teaspoon sugar
1 tablespoon cornstarch
1 teaspoon chicken bouillon granules
¼ teaspoon ground ginger
1 cup water
1 tablespoon reduced-sodium soy sauce
1 tablespoon dry sherry

Combine all ingredients in a heavy saucepan. Place over medium heat, and bring to a boil; boil 1 minute, stirring constantly. **Yield: 1 cup.**

PER SERVING: 400 CALORIES (10% FROM FAT)
FAT 4.3G (SATURATED FAT 1.1G)
PROTEIN 34.3G CARBOHYDRATE 56.2G
CHOLESTEROL 72MG SODIUM 743MG

Chicken with Mole Sauce

2½ cups no-salt-added chicken broth, divided
½ cup onion slices, separated into rings
1 clove garlic, sliced
½ cup raisins
¼ cup slivered almonds
3 tablespoons chili powder
2 tablespoons sesame seeds
1 tablespoon unsweetened cocoa
1 tablespoon sugar
½ teaspoon ground allspice
¼ teaspoon salt
¼ teaspoon pepper
1 tablespoon cornmeal
Vegetable cooking spray
8 (4-ounce) skinned and boned chicken breast
   halves

Combine 2 cups chicken broth, onion, and garlic in a saucepan; cook over medium heat 10 minutes or until onion is tender. Pour into container of an electric blender; add raisins and next 8 ingredients.

Process until smooth, stopping once to scrape down sides. Return mixture to saucepan; stir in cornmeal. Cook over medium heat, stirring constantly, until thickened and bubbly. Remove from heat, and keep sauce warm.

Coat a large nonstick skillet with cooking spray; place over high heat until hot. Add chicken; brown quickly on both sides. Reduce heat; add remaining ½ cup chicken broth, and cook 15 minutes or until chicken is tender.

Spoon ¼ cup sauce onto each plate; place a chicken breast over sauce. **Yield: 8 servings.**

PER SERVING: 232 CALORIES (25% FROM FAT)
FAT 6.5G (SATURATED FAT 1.3G)
PROTEIN 28.6G CARBOHYDRATE 14.1G
CHOLESTEROL 72MG SODIUM 169MG

Chicken-Fried Wild Rice

1 **pound skinned and boned chicken breasts**
¼ **cup low-sodium teriyaki sauce**
¼ **cup low-sodium soy sauce**
¼ **cup Chablis or other dry white wine**
2 **cloves garlic, minced**
½ **teaspoon grated fresh ginger**
¼ **teaspoon Chinese five-spice powder**
1 **(4-ounce) package wild rice**
1 **teaspoon vegetable oil**
1 **cup sliced green pepper**
⅔ **cup sliced carrot**
⅔ **cup chopped onion**
⅔ **cup sliced fresh mushrooms**
½ **cup frozen English peas, thawed**
Vegetable cooking spray
2 **tablespoons slivered almonds, toasted**

Cut chicken into 1-inch pieces; place in a bowl. Add teriyaki sauce and next 5 ingredients; stir well. Cover and marinate in refrigerator at least 1 hour.

Cook rice according to package directions, omitting salt; keep warm.

Add oil to a wok or heavy skillet, and heat to medium-high (375°) for 1 minute. Add green pepper, carrot, and onion; stir-fry 3 minutes. Add mushrooms and peas; stir-fry 2 minutes. Stir into rice; set aside.

Coat wok with cooking spray; place over medium-high heat until hot. Add chicken and marinade to wok; stir-fry 4 minutes or until done. Add rice and vegetables; stir-fry 1 to 2 minutes or until heated. Sprinkle with almonds. **Yield: 4 servings.**

PER SERVING: 317 CALORIES (14% FROM FAT)
FAT 4.9G (SATURATED FAT 0.8G)
PROTEIN 33.6G CARBOHYDRATE 33.4G
CHOLESTEROL 66MG SODIUM 526MG

Chicken-Fried Wild Rice

Chinese Chicken Stir-Fry

1 egg white
1 tablespoon dry sherry
1 teaspoon cornstarch
4 (3-ounce) skinned and boned chicken breast
    halves
3 tablespoons reduced-sodium soy sauce
2 tablespoons water
1 tablespoon rice wine
1½ teaspoons cornstarch
¼ teaspoon salt
2 teaspoons sesame oil
Vegetable cooking spray
2 tablespoons vegetable oil
1 (16-ounce) package frozen broccoli, green
    beans, pearl onions, and red peppers
1 (8-ounce) can bamboo shoots, drained
1 (6-ounce) package frozen snow pea pods
3 cups hot cooked rice (cooked without salt
    or fat)

Combine first 3 ingredients; beat with a wire whisk until frothy. Add chicken; cover and let stand at least 15 minutes.

Combine soy sauce and next 5 ingredients; beat with wire whisk. Set aside.

Coat a wok or heavy skillet with cooking spray; add vegetable oil, and heat to medium-high (375°) for 2 minutes. Add chicken; stir-fry 2 to 3 minutes. Remove chicken from wok.

Add mixed vegetables, bamboo shoots, and snow peas to wok; stir-fry 3 to 4 minutes.

Add chicken and soy sauce mixture; stir-fry until vegetables are crisp-tender. Serve over rice. **Yield: 4 servings.**

PER SERVING: 469 CALORIES (22% FROM FAT)
FAT 11.4G (SATURATED FAT 2.0G)
PROTEIN 29.9G CARBOHYDRATE 60.1G
CHOLESTEROL 49MG SODIUM 635MG

Grilled Lime Chicken with Black Bean Sauce

4 (4-ounce) skinned and boned chicken breast
    halves
¼ cup lime juice
2 tablespoons vegetable oil
½ teaspoon ground red pepper
6 cloves garlic, minced
½ cup finely chopped sweet red pepper
1 tablespoon finely chopped purple onion
1 cup canned black beans, rinsed
½ cup orange juice
2 tablespoons balsamic vinegar
¼ teaspoon salt
⅛ teaspoon freshly ground black pepper
1 clove garlic, minced

Place chicken in a shallow dish; set aside.

Combine lime juice and next 3 ingredients; divide mixture in half. Cover one portion and chill; pour remaining portion over chicken, turning to coat.

Cover chicken, and chill 1 hour.

Combine sweet red pepper and onion in a 9-inch microwave-safe pieplate; cover with wax paper. Microwave at HIGH 1 minute; set aside.

Position knife blade in food processor bowl; add black beans and remaining ingredients. Process 1 minute or until smooth.

Pour black bean mixture into a heavy saucepan, and cook over medium heat until mixture is hot. Keep warm.

Uncover chicken; drain, discarding marinade. Cook chicken, without grill lid, over medium-hot coals (350° to 400°) about 5 minutes on each side or until done, basting with chilled marinade.

Serve chicken with black bean sauce and sweet red pepper mixture. **Yield: 4 servings.**

PER SERVING: 255 CALORIES (24% FROM FAT)
FAT 6.8G (SATURATED FAT 1.5G)
PROTEIN 30.4G CARBOHYDRATE 17.5G
CHOLESTEROL 70MG SODIUM 334MG

Basil-Stuffed Chicken with Tomato-Basil Pasta

4 (4-ounce) skinned and boned chicken breast halves
¼ teaspoon salt
¼ teaspoon garlic powder
2 bunches fresh basil (about 20 large basil leaves)
Tomato-Basil Pasta
Garnish: fresh basil sprigs

Place chicken between 2 sheets of heavy-duty plastic wrap; flatten to ¼-inch thickness, using a meat mallet or rolling pin.

Sprinkle evenly with salt and garlic powder.

Arrange basil leaves in a single layer over chicken. Starting at short end, roll up 2 chicken breasts. Place each roll on top of a remaining chicken breast, and roll up, forming two larger rolls. Secure chicken with wooden picks.

Cook, covered with grill lid, over medium-hot coals (350° to 400°) 18 to 20 minutes, turning once. Wrap in aluminum foil; chill at least 8 hours.

Unwrap chicken rolls, and place on a microwave-safe plate; cover with wax paper.

Microwave at MEDIUM-HIGH (70% power) 1½ minutes, turning once. Remove wooden picks.

Cut each chicken roll into thin slices. Serve slices with Tomato-Basil Pasta. Garnish, if desired. **Yield: 4 servings.**

Tomato-Basil Pasta

1 tablespoon reduced-calorie margarine
2 cloves garlic, minced
¼ cup lemon juice
¼ cup Chablis or other dry white wine
¼ cup chopped fresh basil
1 cup peeled, seeded, and finely chopped tomato
8 ounces thin spaghetti, cooked without salt or fat

Melt margarine in a large saucepan over medium heat; add minced garlic, and cook 1 minute, stirring constantly. Add lemon juice and remaining ingredients; toss gently. **Yield: 4 servings.**

PER SERVING: 387 CALORIES (13% FROM FAT)
FAT 5.4G (SATURATED FAT 1.2G)
PROTEIN 33.7G CARBOHYDRATE 46.7G
CHOLESTEROL 70MG SODIUM 252MG

Sherried Chicken with Artichokes

6 (4-ounce) skinned and boned chicken breast halves
½ teaspoon pepper
1 teaspoon paprika
Vegetable cooking spray
1 (14-ounce) can artichoke hearts, drained
1⅓ cups sliced fresh mushrooms
3 tablespoons thinly sliced green onions
1 tablespoon cornstarch
1 teaspoon chicken-flavored bouillon granules
⅔ cup water
¼ cup dry sherry
½ teaspoon dried rosemary, crushed

Sprinkle chicken with pepper and paprika; set aside. Coat a large nonstick skillet with cooking spray; heat skillet. Add chicken, and cook 5 minutes or until browned, turning once.

Place chicken in a 13- x 9- x 2-inch baking dish coated with cooking spray. Arrange artichoke hearts around chicken; set aside.

Combine mushrooms and green onions in a skillet; cook 5 minutes or until vegetables are tender.

Combine cornstarch and remaining ingredients; stir well. Pour into skillet, and bring to a boil; boil 1 minute, stirring constantly. Pour over chicken mixture. Cover and bake at 375° for 30 minutes. **Yield: 6 servings.**

PER SERVING: 161 CALORIES (11% FROM FAT)
FAT 1.9G (SATURATED FAT 0.5G)
PROTEIN 28.1G CARBOHYDRATE 7.5G
CHOLESTEROL 66MG SODIUM 348MG

Chicken Breasts with Fruited Rice Pilaf

½ cup unsweetened apple juice
½ cup no-salt-added chicken broth
1 cup chopped dried apricots
¼ cup raisins
Butter-flavored cooking spray
1 cup chopped onion
½ cup chopped celery
½ cup chopped fresh parsley
2 cups cooked brown rice (cooked without salt or fat)
½ teaspoon salt
½ teaspoon pepper
½ teaspoon rubbed sage
¼ teaspoon poultry seasoning
4 (6-ounce) skinned chicken breast halves
¼ teaspoon pepper

Combine juice and broth in a saucepan; bring to a boil. Stir in apricots and raisins; remove from heat. Cover and let stand 1 hour. (Do not drain.)

Coat a nonstick skillet with cooking spray; place over medium-high heat until hot. Add onion, celery, and parsley; cook, stirring constantly, until tender. Remove from heat; stir in apricot mixture, rice, and next 4 ingredients.

Place chicken in an 11- x 7- x 1½-inch baking dish coated with cooking spray; sprinkle with ¼ teaspoon pepper. Spoon rice around chicken.

Cover and bake at 350° for 35 minutes; uncover and bake 10 minutes or until chicken is tender. **Yield: 4 servings.**

PER SERVING: 401 CALORIES (7% FROM FAT)
FAT 3.1G (SATURATED FAT 0.6G)
PROTEIN 31.4G CARBOHYDRATE 63.6G
CHOLESTEROL 66MG SODIUM 423MG

Old-Fashioned Chicken and Dumplings

1 (3½-pound) broiler-fryer, cut up and skinned
1 stalk celery, cut into thirds
1 medium onion, quartered
2 quarts water
1 teaspoon salt
½ teaspoon pepper
2 cups all-purpose flour
½ teaspoon baking soda
½ teaspoon salt
3 tablespoons margarine
2 tablespoons chopped fresh parsley
¾ cup nonfat buttermilk

Combine first 5 ingredients in a Dutch oven; bring to a boil. Cover, reduce heat, and simmer 1 hour or until chicken is tender. Remove chicken, reserving broth in Dutch oven; discard vegetables. Let chicken and broth cool.

Bone and cut chicken into bite-size pieces. Place chicken and broth in separate containers; cover and chill 8 hours. Remove fat from broth; bring to a boil, and add pepper.

Combine flour, soda, and ½ teaspoon salt; cut in margarine with a pastry blender until mixture is crumbly. Add parsley and buttermilk, stirring with a fork until dry ingredients are moistened.

Turn dough out onto a heavily floured surface, and knead lightly 4 or 5 times. Pat dough to ¼-inch thickness. Pinch off 1½-inch pieces, and drop into boiling broth. Add chicken. Reduce heat to medium-low, and cook 8 to 10 minutes, stirring occasionally. **Yield: 8 servings.**

PER SERVING: 283 CALORIES (27% FROM FAT)
FAT 8.5G (SATURATED FAT 1.3G)
PROTEIN 20.6G CARBOHYDRATE 26.8G
CHOLESTEROL 50MG SODIUM 613MG

Chicken à la King

Chicken à la King

1 tablespoon reduced-calorie margarine
3 (4-ounce) skinned and boned chicken breast
    halves, cut into bite-size pieces
¼ cup chopped onion
¼ cup sliced fresh mushrooms
¼ cup all-purpose flour
2 cups skim milk
¼ cup frozen English peas, thawed
1 (2-ounce) jar diced pimiento, drained
½ teaspoon salt
½ teaspoon pepper
4 slices wheat bread, trimmed and toasted
¼ teaspoon paprika

Melt margarine in a large nonstick skillet over medium heat. Add chicken and onion; cook, stirring constantly, 3 to 5 minutes or until chicken is browned. Add mushrooms; cook 1 minute.

Stir in flour, and cook, stirring constantly, 1 minute. Gradually add milk and next 4 ingredients; cook over medium heat, stirring constantly, until mixture is thickened and bubbly.

Cut each slice of bread into 4 triangles; serve chicken mixture with 4 toast triangles; sprinkle with paprika. **Yield: 4 servings.**

PER SERVING: 254 CALORIES (14% FROM FAT)
FAT 4.0G (SATURATED FAT 0.6G)
PROTEIN 28.0G CARBOHYDRATE 26.4G
CHOLESTEROL 53MG SODIUM 573MG

Chicken Pot Pie

1 (3½-pound) broiler-fryer
2 quarts water
½ teaspoon salt
½ teaspoon pepper
1 stalk celery, cut into 2-inch pieces
1 medium onion, quartered
1 bay leaf
3½ cups peeled and cubed potato
    (1½ pounds)
1 (16-ounce) package frozen mixed vegetables
½ cup all-purpose flour
1 cup skim milk
¾ teaspoon salt
1 teaspoon pepper
½ teaspoon poultry seasoning
Butter-flavored cooking spray
5 sheets frozen phyllo pastry, thawed

Combine first 7 ingredients in a large Dutch oven; bring to a boil. Cover, reduce heat, and simmer 1 hour or until chicken is tender.

Remove chicken, reserving broth in Dutch oven; discard vegetables and bay leaf. Let chicken cool; skin, bone, and cut into bite-size pieces.

Remove fat (oily liquid) from chicken broth, reserving 3½ cups broth.

Bring reserved broth to a boil in Dutch oven. Add potato and mixed vegetables; return to a boil. Cover, reduce heat, and simmer 8 minutes or until vegetables are tender.

Combine flour and milk in a jar; cover tightly, and shake vigorously. Gradually add to broth mixture in a slow, steady stream, stirring constantly. Cook, stirring constantly, 1 minute or until thickened. Stir in ¾ teaspoon salt, 1 teaspoon pepper, poultry seasoning, and chicken.

Spoon mixture into a 13- x 9- x 2-inch baking dish coated with cooking spray; set aside.

Place 1 phyllo sheet horizontally on a flat surface, keeping remaining sheets covered with a slightly damp towel until ready for use. Coat sheet with cooking spray. Layer remaining 4 sheets on first sheet, coating each with cooking spray. Place on top of baking dish, loosely crushing edges around the dish.

Bake pot pie at 400° for 20 minutes. **Yield: 8 servings.**

Note: Remove fat by chilling broth and removing congealed fat, or by pouring broth through a large fat separator.

PER SERVING: 249 CALORIES (20% FROM FAT)
FAT 5.5G (SATURATED FAT 1.0G)
PROTEIN 21.5G CARBOHYDRATE 25.9G
CHOLESTEROL 50MG SODIUM 465MG

Game Hens with Chutney-Mustard Glaze

1 (1¼-pound) Cornish hen, skinned and split
Vegetable cooking spray
2 tablespoons chopped mango chutney
2 teaspoons Dijon mustard

Place hen halves, cut side down, on a rack coated with cooking spray; place rack in a broiler pan. Combine chutney and mustard, and brush about one-third of chutney mixture over hen.

Bake, uncovered, at 325° for 50 to 60 minutes, brushing twice with chutney mixture. **Yield: 2 servings.**

PER SERVING: 288 CALORIES (30% FROM FAT)
FAT 9.6G (SATURATED FAT 4.3G)
PROTEIN 37.0G CARBOHYDRATE 11.0G
CHOLESTEROL 113MG SODIUM 209MG

Lean Tips for Poultry

- Trim away all visible fat.
- Remove skin either before cooking or before serving.
- Remember that white meat generally contains less fat than dark meat.

Tarragon Roasted Cornish Hens with Vegetables

2 (1¼-pound) Cornish hens, skinned and split
1 teaspoon olive oil
1 tablespoon minced garlic
3 to 4 tablespoons chopped fresh tarragon
1 tablespoon cracked black pepper
½ teaspoon salt
8 Roma tomatoes, halved
4 carrots, cut into 2-inch slices
2 medium onions, quartered
¾ pound fresh mushrooms
1 teaspoon olive oil
½ teaspoon ground white pepper
1 cup Chablis or other dry white wine
1 cup fat-free, reduced-sodium chicken broth
1 teaspoon reduced-sodium Worcestershire sauce
2 dashes of hot sauce

Rub hens with 1 teaspoon olive oil and minced garlic; place hens in a large roasting pan; set aside.

Combine tarragon, black pepper, and salt; sprinkle over hens.

Combine tomato and next 5 ingredients; toss mixture gently, and place in roasting pan.

Bake hens and vegetables at 350° for 45 minutes; keep warm.

Combine pan juices, wine, and remaining ingredients; bring mixture to a boil. Reduce heat, and simmer 20 minutes or until mixture is reduced to 1 cup.

Transfer hens and vegetables to individual serving plates. Serve sauce with hen halves and vegetables. **Yield: 4 servings.**

PER SERVING: 335 CALORIES (20% FROM FAT)
FAT 7.4G (SATURATED FAT 1.7G)
PROTEIN 41.0G CARBOHYDRATE 27.1G
CHOLESTEROL 117MG SODIUM 474MG

Turkey Lasagna

Vegetable cooking spray
1½ pounds freshly ground raw turkey
1¼ cups chopped onion
1 cup chopped green pepper
2 cloves garlic, chopped
½ teaspoon dried Italian seasoning
¼ cup chopped fresh parsley
2 (6-ounce) cans tomato paste
1 (10-ounce) can diced tomatoes and green chiles, undrained
1½ cups water
2 egg whites, lightly beaten
2 cups 1% low-fat cottage cheese
2 tablespoons chopped fresh parsley
10 lasagna noodles, cooked without salt or fat
½ cup grated Parmesan cheese
1 cup (4 ounces) shredded part-skim mozzarella cheese

Coat a large, nonstick skillet with cooking spray; place over medium-high heat until hot. Add ground turkey and next 3 ingredients; cook until meat is browned and vegetables are tender, stirring to crumble meat. Drain and pat dry with paper towels. Wipe drippings from skillet.

Return mixture to skillet; add Italian seasoning and next 4 ingredients. Cover and cook over medium heat 30 minutes, stirring often; set aside. Combine egg whites and next 2 ingredients; set aside.

Coat a 13- x 9- x 2-inch baking dish with cooking spray. Place 5 cooked noodles in bottom of dish. Top with half each of turkey mixture and cottage cheese mixture. Repeat layers.

Cover and bake at 350° for 25 minutes. Uncover and sprinkle with cheeses; bake, uncovered, 5 minutes or until cheese melts. Let stand 10 minutes. **Yield: 8 servings.**

PER SERVING: 369 CALORIES (21% FROM FAT)
FAT 8.5G (SATURATED FAT 3.9G)
PROTEIN 37.6G CARBOHYDRATE 35.1G
CHOLESTEROL 62MG SODIUM 594MG

Turkey-Vegetable Pizza

Turkey-Vegetable Pizza

½ cup no-salt-added tomato sauce
1 (6-ounce) can tomato paste
2 tablespoons grated Parmesan cheese
¾ teaspoon dried Italian seasoning
½ teaspoon dried basil
¼ teaspoon garlic powder
1 teaspoon sugar
⅛ teaspoon ground black pepper
½ pound freshly ground raw turkey
Dash of ground red pepper
¼ teaspoon fennel seeds, crushed
Special Pizza Crust
1 (4-ounce) can sliced mushrooms, drained
¼ cup thinly sliced onion
1 green pepper, cut into strips
1 cup thinly sliced fresh broccoli
1 cup (4 ounces) shredded part-skim
   mozzarella cheese

Combine first 8 ingredients in a bowl; stir well. Let stand 1 hour.

Cook ground turkey, red pepper, and fennel seeds in a nonstick skillet, stirring constantly to crumble meat; drain.

Spread sauce over Special Pizza Crust. Sprinkle turkey mixture over sauce. Top with mushrooms, onion, green pepper, and broccoli.

Bake at 425° for 15 minutes. Top with cheese; bake 5 minutes. **Yield: 8 servings.**

Special Pizza Crust

½ package active dry yeast
2 tablespoons warm water
½ cup whole wheat flour
½ cup all-purpose flour
⅛ teaspoon salt
1½ teaspoons olive oil
¼ to ⅓ cup warm water
Vegetable cooking spray

Dissolve yeast in 2 tablespoons warm water in a small bowl; let stand 5 minutes. Combine flours and salt in a large bowl; stir in yeast mixture and oil. Add enough warm water to make a moderately stiff dough; stir well. Cover; let stand 15 minutes.

Turn dough out onto a lightly floured surface. Knead 5 to 8 times.

Roll dough into a 12-inch circle; place on a 12-inch pizza pan coated with cooking spray.

Bake at 425° for 5 minutes. **Yield: 1 (12-inch) pizza crust.**

PER SERVING: 169 CALORIES (24% FROM FAT)
FAT 4.7G (SATURATED FAT 2.1G)
PROTEIN 12.6G CARBOHYDRATE 20.6G
CHOLESTEROL 23MG SODIUM 164MG

Oven-Fried Turkey Cutlets

1 large egg
2 teaspoons vegetable oil
½ cup Italian-seasoned breadcrumbs
2 tablespoons grated Parmesan cheese
1 pound turkey breast cutlets
Vegetable cooking spray
½ cup commercial marinara sauce

Combine egg and oil in a shallow dish; beat well, and set aside.

Combine breadcrumbs and Parmesan cheese in a shallow dish. Dip turkey in egg mixture; dredge in breadcrumb mixture.

Place turkey on a baking sheet coated with cooking spray. Spray each cutlet lightly with cooking spray.

Bake at 350° for 8 to 10 minutes or until done. Serve turkey with marinara sauce. **Yield: 4 servings.**

PER SERVING: 260 CALORIES (27% FROM FAT)
FAT 7.8G (SATURATED FAT 2.2G)
PROTEIN 32.0G CARBOHYDRATE 14.1G
CHOLESTEROL 125MG SODIUM 747MG

Turkey-and-Shrimp Florentine Casserole

1 pound unpeeled medium-size fresh shrimp
1 pound turkey breast fillets
¼ teaspoon garlic powder
¼ teaspoon pepper
¼ cup Chablis or other dry white wine
2 (10-ounce) packages frozen chopped spinach
1 (8-ounce) container light process cream cheese
1 (10¾-ounce) can 99% fat-free cream of mushroom soup, undiluted
3 tablespoons Parmesan cheese
Vegetable cooking spray
2 tablespoons fine, dry breadcrumbs

Peel and devein shrimp; set aside. Sprinkle turkey with garlic powder and pepper; set aside.

Place wine in a large, nonstick skillet; add turkey, and bring to a boil. Add shrimp; cover, reduce heat, and cook 3 to 5 minutes or until shrimp turn pink. Remove from heat; cool slightly. Drain pan juices, and set aside. Cut turkey into bite-size pieces, and set turkey and shrimp aside.

Cook spinach according to package directions, omitting salt; drain well between layers of paper towels.

Place cream cheese in a large saucepan; cook over low heat, stirring constantly, until cheese melts. Remove from heat; stir in reserved pan juices, mushroom soup, Parmesan cheese, and spinach. Gently stir in turkey and shrimp.

Spoon mixture into an 11- x 7- x 1½-inch baking dish coated with cooking spray; sprinkle with breadcrumbs.

Bake at 350° for 35 to 45 minutes or until bubbly. **Yield: 6 servings.**

Note: Cover and freeze casserole before sprinkling with breadcrumbs. Thaw in refrigerator 24 hours; let stand at room temperature 30 minutes.

Sprinkle with breadcrumbs, and bake at 350° for 35 to 45 minutes or until bubbly.

PER SERVING: 296 CALORIES (31% FROM FAT)
FAT 10.3G (SATURATED FAT 4.8G)
PROTEIN 37.3G CARBOHYDRATE 12.7G
CHOLESTEROL 157MG SODIUM 664MG

Lazy Day Turkey

1½ tablespoons butter-flavored mix
¼ cup water
½ cup chopped onion
½ cup chopped green pepper
½ cup sliced fresh mushrooms
1 clove garlic, minced
2 cups cubed, cooked turkey breast
1 (10¾-ounce) can ready-to-serve, reduced-fat cream of chicken soup
½ cup skim milk
2 tablespoons no-sugar-added apricot spread
1 tablespoon dry white wine
¼ teaspoon salt
¼ teaspoon ground nutmeg
¼ teaspoon pepper
4 cups hot cooked rice or pasta (cooked without salt or fat)

Combine butter-flavored mix and water, stirring until mix dissolves. Pour into a large skillet; add onion and next 3 ingredients. Cook over medium heat, stirring constantly, until vegetables are tender.

Stir in turkey and next 7 ingredients; bring mixture to a boil over medium heat. Reduce heat, and simmer, uncovered, 10 to 15 minutes, stirring occasionally.

Serve over rice or pasta. **Yield: 4 servings.**

PER SERVING: 386 CALORIES (6% FROM FAT)
FAT 2.6G (SATURATED FAT 0.3G)
PROTEIN 27.6G CARBOHYDRATE 58.7G
CHOLESTEROL 63MG SODIUM 660MG

Salads

These salads will help make meals appetizing as well as nutritious. We begin with side salads followed by protein-rich treasures substantial enough for a main dish.

Apple-Apricot Salad, Frozen Strawberry Salad, Rice-Shrimp Salad

Asparagus Salad, Sunburst Chicken-and-Walnut Salad, Crab-and-Asparagus Salad

Creamy Potato Salad, Minted Marinated Fruit, Marinated Black-Eyed Pea Salad

Citrus Spinach Salad, Green Beans with Creamy Tarragon Dressing

Three-Layer Aspic (page 108)

Three-Layer Aspic

(pictured on page 107)

1 envelope unflavored gelatin
¼ cup water
1 tablespoon lemon juice
1 (8-ounce) carton plain low-fat yogurt
Vegetable cooking spray
1 envelope unflavored gelatin
1 cup water
1 tablespoon lemon juice
1 teaspoon reduced-sodium Worcestershire
    sauce
1 cup diced green pepper
1 (14½-ounce) can stewed tomatoes,
    undrained
1 (12-ounce) can vegetable cocktail juice
1 tablespoon sugar
1 teaspoon celery salt
1 teaspoon reduced-sodium Worcestershire
    sauce
¼ teaspoon hot sauce
2 tablespoons lemon juice
1 bay leaf
2 envelopes unflavored gelatin
1 cup thinly sliced celery
Lettuce leaves
Garnish: lemon slices

Sprinkle 1 envelope gelatin over ¼ cup water in a small saucepan; let stand 1 minute. Cook over medium heat, stirring constantly, until gelatin dissolves; remove from heat.

Stir in 1 tablespoon lemon juice and yogurt. Pour into a 6-cup mold that has been coated with cooking spray; cover and chill until firm.

Sprinkle 1 envelope gelatin over 1 cup water in a small saucepan; let stand 1 minute. Cook over medium heat, stirring constantly, until gelatin dissolves; remove from heat.

Stir in 1 tablespoon lemon juice and 1 teaspoon Worcestershire sauce; chill until the consistency of unbeaten egg white. Stir in green pepper. Spoon over yogurt layer. Cover; chill.

Drain tomatoes, reserving liquid; chop tomatoes. Combine liquid, tomatoes, vegetable juice, and next 6 ingredients in a saucepan. Cook over low heat 30 minutes; remove from heat.

Remove bay leaf. Sprinkle 2 envelopes gelatin over hot mixture; stir until gelatin dissolves.

Chill until the consistency of unbeaten egg white. Stir in celery; spoon over green pepper layer. Cover; chill. Unmold onto lettuce leaves. Garnish, if desired. **Yield: 12 (½-cup) servings.**

PER SERVING: 50 CALORIES (11% FROM FAT)
FAT 0.6G (SATURATED FAT 0.2G)
PROTEIN 4.0G CARBOHYDRATE 7.9G
CHOLESTEROL 1MG SODIUM 396MG

Apple-Apricot Salad

1 envelope unflavored gelatin
2 cups unsweetened apple juice, divided
2 teaspoons lemon juice
1½ cups chopped apple
8 canned apricot halves in extra-light syrup,
    drained and chopped
Vegetable cooking spray
Lettuce leaves
Garnish: apple wedges

Sprinkle gelatin over 1 cup apple juice in a small saucepan; let stand 1 minute. Cook over medium heat, stirring constantly, until gelatin dissolves; remove from heat.

Add remaining apple juice and lemon juice. Chill until the consistency of unbeaten egg white.

Fold in apple and apricots; spoon into 7 (½-cup) molds coated with cooking spray. Cover and chill until firm.

Unmold onto lettuce-lined plates. Garnish, if desired. **Yield: 7 (½-cup) servings.**

PER SERVING: 77 CALORIES (5% FROM FAT)
FAT 0.4G (SATURATED FAT 0.0G)
PROTEIN 1.4G CARBOHYDRATE 17.9G
CHOLESTEROL 0MG SODIUM 7MG

Apple-Apricot Salad

Frozen Strawberry Salad

1 (8-ounce) package nonfat cream cheese,
    softened
½ cup sugar
1 (8-ounce) container reduced-fat frozen
    whipped topping, thawed
2 cups frozen no-sugar-added whole
    strawberries, thawed and halved
1 (15¼-ounce) can unsweetened crushed
    pineapple, undrained
1½ cups sliced banana (2 medium)

Beat cream cheese at medium speed of an electric mixer until creamy; gradually add sugar, beating until smooth.

Fold in whipped topping and remaining ingredients; spoon into a 13- x 9- x 2-inch dish.

Cover and freeze until firm. **Yield: 12 servings.**

PER SERVING: 138 CALORIES (17% FROM FAT)
FAT 2.6G (SATURATED FAT 0.0G)
PROTEIN 3.7G CARBOHYDRATE 25.9G
CHOLESTEROL 4MG SODIUM 128MG

Minted Marinated Fruit

1 (20-ounce) can unsweetened pineapple
    chunks, undrained
1½ cups unpeeled, chopped red apple
1½ cups unpeeled, chopped green apple
1 cup unpeeled, chopped pear
1 cup sliced banana
½ cup orange juice
2 tablespoons chopped fresh mint
1 tablespoon honey

Drain pineapple chunks, reserving juice. Combine fruit in an 11- x 7- x 1½-inch dish.

Combine reserved pineapple juice, orange juice, and remaining ingredients; pour over fruit. Cover and chill 3 hours, stirring occasionally. **Yield: 7 (1-cup) servings.**

PER SERVING: 129 CALORIES (3% FROM FAT)
FAT 0.4G (SATURATED FAT 0.1G)
PROTEIN 0.5G CARBOHYDRATE 32.6G
CHOLESTEROL 0MG SODIUM 1MG

Cabbage-Pineapple Slaw

1 (8-ounce) can unsweetened pineapple
    tidbits, undrained
3 cups finely shredded cabbage
1½ cups unpeeled, chopped Red Delicious
    apple
½ cup chopped celery
¼ cup golden raisins
¼ cup reduced-calorie mayonnaise
Lettuce leaves
Garnishes: apple wedges, celery leaves

Drain pineapple, reserving 3 tablespoons juice. Combine pineapple, cabbage, and next 3 ingredients in a large bowl.

Combine reserved pineapple juice and mayonnaise; add to cabbage mixture, tossing gently. Cover and chill. Spoon into a lettuce-lined bowl and garnish, if desired. **Yield: 5 (1-cup) servings.**

PER SERVING: 115 CALORIES (27% FROM FAT)
FAT 3.5G (SATURATED FAT 0.5G)
PROTEIN 1.3G CARBOHYDRATE 21.3G
CHOLESTEROL 4MG SODIUM 110MG

Cleaning Greens

• Wash and dry salad greens before using or storing them. (A salad spinner is useful.)
• Loosely wrap clean greens in paper towels, and store in an airtight container in crisper drawer of the refrigerator. Tear, rather than cut, for salads.

Cabbage-Pineapple Slaw and Parmesan-Stuffed Tomatoes (page 139)

Marinated Black-Eyed Pea Salad and Green Beans with Creamy Tarragon Dressing

Green Beans with Creamy Tarragon Dressing

1½ pounds fresh green beans
1 cup nonfat mayonnaise
⅓ cup chopped fresh parsley
¼ cup chopped onion
¼ cup 1% low-fat cottage cheese
3 tablespoons tarragon vinegar
2 tablespoons skim milk
1½ teaspoons lemon juice
½ teaspoon anchovy paste
Belgian endive, sliced

Wash beans; trim ends, if desired, and remove strings. Arrange beans in a steamer basket, and place over boiling water. Cover and steam 12 minutes or until crisp-tender. Remove beans, and plunge into ice water. Drain; cover and chill.

Position knife blade in food processor bowl; add mayonnaise and next 7 ingredients. Process 1 minute or until smooth, stopping once to scrape down sides. Cover and chill at least 1 hour.

Arrange endive on individual plates; place beans in center of plates, and top each serving with ½ tablespoon dressing. **Yield: 6 servings.**

Note: When preparing young, tender green beans, trim the stem end only, leaving the pointed end of beans on to enhance the appearance and fiber content of the salad.

PER SERVING: 84 CALORIES (4% FROM FAT)
FAT 0.4G (SATURATED FAT 0.1G)
PROTEIN 3.9G CARBOHYDRATE 18.0G
CHOLESTEROL 0MG SODIUM 615MG

Marinated Black-Eyed Pea Salad

1½ cups water
1 medium onion, halved
½ teaspoon salt
½ teaspoon dried crushed red pepper
⅛ teaspoon hickory-flavored liquid smoke
1 (16-ounce) package frozen black-eyed peas
½ cup raspberry wine vinegar
¼ cup water
3 tablespoons chopped fresh parsley
1 clove garlic, minced
1 teaspoon olive oil
¼ teaspoon salt
¼ teaspoon freshly ground pepper
½ cup chopped sweet red pepper
⅓ cup small purple onion rings
Leaf lettuce
¾ cup croutons

Combine first 5 ingredients in a saucepan; bring to a boil. Add peas; return to a boil. Cover, reduce heat, and simmer 40 to 45 minutes or until peas are tender. Remove and discard onion; drain. Rinse with cold water; drain. Place in a bowl; set aside.

Combine vinegar and next 7 ingredients. Pour over peas; toss to coat. Cover; chill 8 hours, stirring occasionally. Stir in purple onion. Serve on lettuce-lined plates. Sprinkle with croutons. **Yield: 5 (¾-cup) servings.**

PER SERVING: 188 CALORIES (14% FROM FAT)
FAT 3.0G (SATURATED FAT 0.3G)
PROTEIN 9.5G CARBOHYDRATE 31.8G
CHOLESTEROL 0MG SODIUM 257MG

Asparagus Salad

1 pound fresh asparagus spears
¼ cup lemon juice
2 tablespoons honey
2 teaspoons vegetable oil
8 lettuce leaves

Snap off tough ends of asparagus. Remove scales from stalks, if desired. Arrange asparagus in a steamer basket; place over boiling water. Cover and steam 6 minutes or until crisp-tender.

Plunge asparagus into ice water to stop the cooking process; drain and chill.

Combine lemon juice, honey, and oil in a jar; cover tightly, and shake vigorously. Chill.

Arrange lettuce leaves on individual plates; top with asparagus, and drizzle with dressing. **Yield: 4 servings.**

PER SERVING: 75 CALORIES (30% FROM FAT)
FAT 2.5G (SATURATED FAT 0.5G)
PROTEIN 1.9G CARBOHYDRATE 13.6G
CHOLESTEROL 0MG SODIUM 5MG

Citrus Spinach Salad

2 tablespoons orange juice
2 tablespoons rice vinegar
2½ teaspoons vegetable oil
1 tablespoon honey
¼ teaspoon grated orange rind
6 cups torn spinach
2 oranges, peeled, seeded, and sectioned
¾ medium-size purple onion, sliced and
    separated into rings

Combine first 5 ingredients in a jar; cover tightly, and shake vigorously. Chill thoroughly. Combine spinach, orange sections, and onion rings in a salad bowl.

Drizzle dressing over spinach mixture; toss gently. **Yield: 6 (1-cup) servings.**

PER SERVING: 73 CALORIES (27% FROM FAT)
FAT 2.2G (SATURATED FAT 0.4G)
PROTEIN 2.3G CARBOHYDRATE 13.1G
CHOLESTEROL 0MG SODIUM 45MG

Creamy Potato Salad

2 pounds unpeeled red potatoes (about 6 medium)
¼ cup chopped green onions
1 (2-ounce) jar diced pimiento, drained
⅓ cup nonfat mayonnaise
¼ cup plain low-fat yogurt
1½ tablespoons prepared mustard
1 tablespoon sugar
1 tablespoon white wine vinegar
½ teaspoon salt
½ teaspoon celery seeds
¼ teaspoon pepper
⅛ teaspoon garlic powder

Place potatoes in a medium saucepan; cover with water, and bring to a boil. Cover, reduce heat, and simmer 25 minutes or until tender; drain and let cool.

Peel potatoes, and cut into ½-inch cubes. Combine potato, green onions, and pimiento in a large bowl.

Combine mayonnaise and remaining ingredients; stir into potato mixture, and toss gently. Cover and chill. **Yield: 10 (½-cup) servings.**

PER SERVING: 86 CALORIES (3% FROM FAT)
FAT 0.3G (SATURATED FAT 0.1G)
PROTEIN 2.5G CARBOHYDRATE 18.9G
CHOLESTEROL 0MG SODIUM 260MG

Lighten Up Potato Salad

Nonfat mayonnaise and low-fat yogurt replace eggs and cream in Creamy Potato Salad. This recipe has less than 1 gram of fat and no cholesterol. For additional fiber, leave the skin on the potatoes.

Sunburst Chicken-and-Walnut Salad

1½ cups water
1 medium onion, halved
1 stalk celery, halved
4 black peppercorns
4 (4-ounce) skinned and boned chicken breast halves
2 tablespoons cider vinegar
2½ teaspoons vegetable oil
2 teaspoons honey
½ teaspoon dry mustard
½ teaspoon dried tarragon
½ teaspoon grated orange rind
2 oranges, peeled and sectioned
8 lettuce leaves
1½ tablespoons chopped walnuts, toasted

Combine first 4 ingredients in a large skillet, and bring to a boil. Cover, reduce heat, and simmer 10 minutes. Place chicken in skillet; cover and simmer 10 minutes or until tender.

Remove chicken, and let cool (discard vegetables, and reserve broth for another use). Cut chicken into strips; set aside.

Combine vinegar and next 5 ingredients in a medium bowl, stirring with a wire whisk. Add orange sections; set aside.

Line each salad plate with 2 lettuce leaves. Remove orange sections from dressing, and divide evenly among plates. Place chicken strips in dressing, and toss gently; divide strips evenly among plates. Drizzle remaining dressing evenly over salads; sprinkle evenly with walnuts. **Yield: 4 servings.**

PER SERVING: 237 CALORIES (30% FROM FAT)
FAT 7.8G (SATURATED FAT 1.5G)
PROTEIN 28.3G CARBOHYDRATE 13.5G
CHOLESTEROL 72MG SODIUM 67MG

Sunburst Chicken-and-Walnut Salad

Crab-and-Asparagus Salad

18 fresh asparagus spears (¾ pound)
¼ cup nonfat mayonnaise
1 tablespoon lemon juice
1 teaspoon chopped capers
½ teaspoon prepared mustard
½ teaspoon white wine Worcestershire sauce
12 large lettuce leaves
¾ pound fresh lump crabmeat, drained
⅛ teaspoon paprika

Snap off tough ends of asparagus. Remove scales from stalks with a vegetable peeler or knife, if desired. Arrange asparagus in a steamer basket over boiling water. Cover and steam 6 minutes or until crisp-tender.

Plunge asparagus into ice water to stop the cooking process; drain and chill.

Combine mayonnaise and next 4 ingredients. Arrange lettuce leaves on individual serving plates; top with equal amounts of asparagus and crabmeat. Serve each salad with 1 tablespoon mayonnaise mixture, and sprinkle with paprika. **Yield: 6 servings.**

PER SERVING: 75 CALORIES (13% FROM FAT)
FAT 1.1G (SATURATED FAT 0.2G)
PROTEIN 11.7G CARBOHYDRATE 4.6G
CHOLESTEROL 52MG SODIUM 323MG

Cooking Shrimp

• Shrimp cooked in its shell is more flavorful than shrimp peeled before cooking. Avoid overcooking shrimp, or it will become tough and rubbery.
• To devein shrimp, cut a shallow slit down the middle of the outside curve. Remove dark vein, and rinse with cold water.

Rice-Shrimp Salad

2 unpeeled, medium tomatoes (¾ pound)
3 cups water
1 pound unpeeled medium-size fresh shrimp
2 cups cooked rice (cooked without salt or fat)
1 cup unpeeled, chopped apple
¾ cup chopped green pepper
½ cup sliced celery
¼ cup chopped green onions
1 tablespoon chopped fresh parsley
3 tablespoons white wine vinegar
1 tablespoon olive oil
½ teaspoon salt
¼ teaspoon pepper
2 cloves garlic, minced
6 red cabbage leaves (optional)
6 lemon wedges (optional)

Cut tomatoes in half. Carefully squeeze each half over a small bowl to remove seeds; pour juice through a wire-mesh strainer into a small bowl, discarding seeds. Reserve 2 tablespoons juice. Chop tomatoes.

Bring water to a boil; add shrimp, and cook 3 to 5 minutes. Drain well, and rinse with cold water. Peel and devein shrimp.

Combine chopped tomato, shrimp, rice, and next 5 ingredients in a large bowl; set aside.

Combine reserved tomato juice, vinegar, and next 4 ingredients; stir with a wire whisk until blended. Pour over shrimp mixture, and toss gently; chill.

Spoon salad over cabbage leaves, and serve with a lemon wedge, if desired. **Yield: 6 (1¼-cup) servings.**

PER SERVING: 170 CALORIES (16% FROM FAT)
FAT 3.1G (SATURATED FAT 0.5G)
PROTEIN 11.2G CARBOHYDRATE 24.1G
CHOLESTEROL 83MG SODIUM 307MG

Rice-Shrimp Salad

Shrimp-and-Rice Salad

(pictured on page 2)

3 cups water
1 pound unpeeled medium-size fresh shrimp
2 cups cooked rice (cooked without salt or fat)
½ cup chopped celery
½ cup chopped green pepper
¼ cup sliced pimiento-stuffed olives
¼ cup chopped onion
2 tablespoons diced pimiento
3 tablespoons commercial oil-free Italian dressing
2 tablespoons reduced-calorie mayonnaise
2 tablespoons prepared mustard
1 tablespoon lemon juice
1 teaspoon salt-free lemon-pepper seasoning
⅛ teaspoon pepper
Lettuce leaves
Garnishes: fresh parsley sprig, cooked shrimp, and pimiento-stuffed olive

Bring water to a boil; add shrimp, and cook 3 to 5 minutes or until shrimp turn pink. Drain well; rinse with cold water. Chill. Peel and devein shrimp.

Combine shrimp, rice, and next 5 ingredients in a medium bowl. Combine Italian dressing and next 5 ingredients, stirring until well blended. Pour over shrimp mixture, and toss gently to coat.

Cover; chill 3 to 4 hours. Line a serving plate with lettuce leaves. Spoon salad onto plate and garnish, if desired. **Yield: 5 (1-cup) servings.**

PER SERVING: 188 CALORIES (15% FROM FAT)
FAT 3.1G (SATURATED FAT 0.5G)
PROTEIN 13.5G CARBOHYDRATE 25.8G
CHOLESTEROL 101MG SODIUM 410MG

Oriental Salmon-and-Wild Rice Salad

1 (8-ounce) fillet fresh salmon
⅓ cup rice wine vinegar
¼ cup orange marmalade
2 tablespoons teriyaki sauce
1 tablespoon grated fresh ginger
2 teaspoons sesame oil
1 (6-ounce) package wild rice, cooked without salt
¾ cup fresh snow pea pods
½ cup sliced green onions
½ cup finely chopped sweet red pepper
Bibb lettuce leaves

Place salmon in an 8-inch square dish, and set aside.

Combine vinegar and next 4 ingredients in a jar; cover tightly, and shake vigorously. Pour half of mixture over salmon, turning to coat well. Set remaining vinegar mixture aside.

Cover salmon, and chill 1 hour.

Drain salmon, discarding marinade; place salmon on a rack in broiler pan.

Broil salmon 5½ inches from heat (with electric oven door partially opened) 3 to 5 minutes on each side or until fish flakes easily when tested with a fork.

Separate salmon into chunks. Cool.

Combine salmon, rice, and next 3 ingredients in a large bowl; drizzle with remaining vinegar mixture, tossing gently.

Cover and chill at least 3 hours. Serve on lettuce leaves. **Yield: 5 (1-cup) servings.**

PER SERVING: 323 CALORIES (18% FROM FAT)
FAT 6.5G (SATURATED FAT 1.0G)
PROTEIN 19.1G CARBOHYDRATE 48.9G
CHOLESTEROL 31MG SODIUM 389MG

Soups & Sandwiches

Let homemade soups and hearty sandwiches solve the what-to-serve dilemma. Use the nutrient grids to help you mix and match recipes to create balanced, light meals.

Light Cream of Broccoli Soup, Corn Chowder, French Onion Soup

Healthy Heroes, Salmon Burgers, Open-Faced Breakfast Sandwiches, Fiesta Burgers

Split Pea Soup, Seafood Chowder, Spicy Ham-and-Bean Soup, Catfish Gumbo

Hot Venison Chili, Smoked Turkey-Roasted Pepper Sandwiches

Beef Stew (page 123)

Light Cream of Broccoli Soup

Light Cream of Broccoli Soup

1 (16-ounce) can ready-to-serve, low-sodium,
    fat-free chicken broth
1/3 cup instant nonfat dry milk powder
3 tablespoons cornstarch
1/2 teaspoon dried onion flakes
1/4 teaspoon salt
1/4 teaspoon dried basil
1/4 teaspoon dried thyme
1/4 teaspoon pepper
1 (10-ounce) package frozen chopped
    broccoli, thawed and drained
1 1/2 cups skim milk
1/3 cup (1.3 ounces) shredded reduced-fat
    Cheddar cheese
1 tablespoon butter-flavored granules
Garnish: shredded reduced-fat Cheddar
    cheese

Combine first 8 ingredients in a large sauce-pan; bring to a boil, stirring constantly. Cook, stirring constantly, 1 minute.

Add broccoli and next 3 ingredients; cook until cheese melts and mixture is thoroughly heated. Garnish individual servings with 1/2 teaspoon shredded Cheddar cheese, if desired. **Yield: 4 (1-cup) servings.**

PER SERVING: 155 CALORIES (13% FROM FAT)
FAT 2.2G (SATURATED FAT 1.2G)
PROTEIN 11.8G CARBOHYDRATE 21.5G
CHOLESTEROL 10MG SODIUM 396MG

Corn Chowder

1/2 cup chopped onion
1/2 cup chopped celery
2 tablespoons reduced-calorie margarine,
    melted
1 tablespoon all-purpose flour
4 cups skim milk
1 (17-ounce) can no-salt-added yellow
    cream-style corn
1/4 teaspoon salt
1/4 teaspoon ground white pepper
1/4 teaspoon dried thyme
1/8 teaspoon paprika

Cook onion and celery in margarine in a Dutch oven until tender, stirring constantly. Add flour, and cook 1 minute, stirring constantly. Gradually add milk, stirring until mixture boils.

Stir in corn and next 3 ingredients. Reduce heat; simmer 20 minutes, stirring occasionally.

Spoon chowder into bowls; sprinkle evenly with paprika. **Yield: 3 (1 2/3-cup) servings.**

PER SERVING: 295 CALORIES (19% FROM FAT)
FAT 6.2G (SATURATED FAT 1.2G)
PROTEIN 14.6G CARBOHYDRATE 49.0G
CHOLESTEROL 7MG SODIUM 462MG

French Onion Soup

2 tablespoons margarine
Vegetable cooking spray
6 large onions, thinly sliced (3 pounds)
2 (10½-ounce) cans beef consommé,
    undiluted
1 (13¾-ounce) can ready-to-serve, no-salt-
    added, fat-free beef-flavored broth
1⅓ cups water
¼ cup Chablis or other dry white wine
¼ teaspoon freshly ground pepper
7 (1-inch-thick) slices French bread
¼ cup grated Parmesan cheese

   Melt margarine in a Dutch oven coated with cooking spray. Add onion, and cook over medium heat, 5 minutes, stirring often. Add 1 can beef consommé; cook over low heat 30 minutes.

   Add remaining beef consommé and next 4 ingredients; bring to a boil, reduce heat, and simmer 10 minutes.

French Onion Soup

   Place bread slices on a baking sheet; sprinkle with Parmesan cheese. Broil 6 inches from heat (with electric oven door partially opened) until cheese is golden. Ladle soup into serving bowls, and top each with a toasted bread slice. **Yield: 7 (1-cup) servings.**

PER SERVING: 247 CALORIES (19% FROM FAT)
FAT 5.2G (SATURATED FAT 1.5G)
PROTEIN 10.3G CARBOHYDRATE 39.0G
CHOLESTEROL 19MG SODIUM 860MG

Split Pea Soup

1 (16-ounce) package dried green split peas
8 cups water
2 bay leaves
1½ teaspoons salt
1 teaspoon dried thyme
3 cloves garlic, minced
¼ cup Chablis or other dry white wine
2 cups sliced carrot
1½ cups diced potato
1 cup chopped celery
¾ cup chopped onion
2 tablespoons dried parsley flakes
2 tablespoons lemon juice

   Combine first 6 ingredients in a Dutch oven. Bring mixture to a boil; reduce heat, and simmer, uncovered, 1 hour.

   Add wine and remaining ingredients to Dutch oven; cook 30 minutes or until peas are tender. Remove bay leaves.

   Spoon mixture into container of an electric blender or food processor; cover and process until mixture is smooth. **Yield: 11 (1-cup) servings.**

PER SERVING: 175 CALORIES (3% FROM FAT)
FAT 0.6G (SATURATED FAT 0.1G)
PROTEIN 11.1G CARBOHYDRATE 32.8G
CHOLESTEROL 0MG SODIUM 345MG

Seafood Chowder

Seafood Chowder

1½ pounds unpeeled medium-size fresh shrimp
Vegetable cooking spray
1 teaspoon olive oil
1 cup chopped onion
1 cup chopped celery
1 cup diced sweet red pepper
3 cloves garlic, minced
½ cup all-purpose flour
2 (10½-ounce) cans ready-to-serve, no-salt-added chicken broth
1½ cups water
3 cups peeled, diced red potato
1 cup diced carrot
½ teaspoon ground white pepper
½ teaspoon dried thyme
2 bay leaves
2 (12-ounce) cans evaporated skimmed milk
2 (8¾-ounce) cans no-salt-added, cream-style corn
1 teaspoon hot sauce
1 pound fresh crabmeat, drained and flaked

Peel and devein shrimp; set aside. Coat a Dutch oven with cooking spray; add oil, and place over medium-high heat until hot. Add onion and next 3 ingredients; cook until tender.

Add flour, and cook, stirring constantly, 1 minute. Gradually stir in chicken broth, water, and next 5 ingredients. Bring to a boil; reduce heat, and simmer, uncovered, 20 minutes or until potato is tender, stirring often.

Stir in milk, corn, and hot sauce; return to a boil. Add reserved shrimp and crabmeat; cook 5 minutes or until shrimp turn pink, stirring constantly. Remove and discard bay leaves. **Yield: 10 (1½-cup) servings.**

Note: Freeze in airtight containers. Thaw in refrigerator 24 hours. Place in a saucepan, and cook over low heat until heated.

PER SERVING: 278 CALORIES (9% FROM FAT)
FAT 2.7G (SATURATED FAT 0.5G)
PROTEIN 27.1G CARBOHYDRATE 35.6G
CHOLESTEROL 123MG SODIUM 296MG

Spicy Ham-and-Bean Soup

1 pound dried Great Northern beans
4 quarts water
1 pound reduced-salt lean ham, trimmed and
    cubed
2 stalks celery, chopped
2 carrots, scraped and chopped
2 medium-size red potatoes, finely chopped
1 large onion, finely chopped
1 tablespoon chopped pickled jalapeño
    pepper
1 tablespoon pickled jalapeño pepper juice
1 (6-ounce) can spicy tomato-vegetable juice
1 (4.5-ounce) can chopped green chiles,
    undrained
1 tablespoon Worcestershire sauce
½ teaspoon chili powder
½ teaspoon garlic powder

    Sort and wash beans; place in a Dutch oven.
Add water, and let stand 2 hours. Bring to a boil;
reduce heat, and simmer 1 hour.
    Add ham and next 4 ingredients; simmer 1
additional hour.
    Add jalapeño pepper and remaining ingredi-
ents; simmer 1 hour or until beans are tender and
soup is thickened. **Yield: 9 (1½-cup) servings.**

PER SERVING: 297 CALORIES (10% FROM FAT)
FAT 3.2G (SATURATED FAT 0.9G)
PROTEIN 21.9G CARBOHYDRATE 46.8G
CHOLESTEROL 25MG SODIUM 528MG

Beef Stew

(pictured on page 119)

1 pound boneless top round steak
¼ cup all-purpose flour
¼ teaspoon pepper
¾ cup chopped onion
1 tablespoon vegetable oil
3 cups water
½ cup finely chopped carrot
¼ cup finely chopped celery
2 tablespoons minced fresh parsley
½ teaspoon salt
⅛ teaspoon dried thyme
2 cups cubed potato
1 cup sliced carrot
1 cup chopped onion
1 cup frozen green peas, thawed

    Trim fat from steak; cut into 1-inch cubes.
Combine flour and pepper; dredge meat in flour
mixture, reserving excess flour mixture.
    Cook meat, ¾ cup onion, and reserved flour
mixture in oil in a Dutch oven over low heat
until meat is lightly browned.
    Add water and next 5 ingredients. Cover,
reduce heat, and simmer 1½ hours.
    Stir in potato, 1 cup carrot, and 1 cup onion;
cover and simmer 20 minutes. Add green peas,
and cook 10 additional minutes. **Yield: 4 (1½-
cup) servings.**

PER SERVING: 338 CALORIES (21% FROM FAT)
FAT 8.0G (SATURATED FAT 2.2G)
PROTEIN 29.7G CARBOHYDRATE 35.4G
CHOLESTEROL 60MG SODIUM 419MG

Freezing Soups

Most soups, stews, chilis, and gumbos freeze well, which is a bonus when you make a large
quantity. When freezing soups, use airtight plastic containers or heavy-duty, zip-top plastic
bags; label and date the item, and use within three or four months for optimum flavor.

Catfish Gumbo

Catfish Gumbo

Vegetable cooking spray
1 cup chopped celery
1 cup chopped onion
1 cup chopped green pepper
2 cloves garlic, minced
3 (10½-ounce) cans ready-to-serve, no-salt-added chicken broth
2 (14½-ounce) cans no-salt-added tomatoes, undrained and chopped
1 (6-ounce) can low-sodium cocktail vegetable juice
2 bay leaves
1½ teaspoons salt
½ teaspoon pepper
½ teaspoon dried thyme
½ teaspoon hot sauce
1½ pounds farm-raised catfish fillets, cut into 1½-inch pieces
2 (10-ounce) packages frozen sliced okra, thawed
4 cups hot cooked rice (cooked without salt or fat)

Coat a Dutch oven with cooking spray; place over medium-high heat until hot. Add celery and next 3 ingredients, stirring constantly until crisp-tender.

Add chicken broth and next 7 ingredients. Bring mixture to a boil; cover, reduce heat, and simmer 30 minutes. Stir in fish and okra; cover and simmer 15 minutes.

Remove and discard bay leaves. Serve gumbo over ½ cup hot cooked rice. **Yield: 8 (1⅓-cup) servings.**

PER SERVING: 283 CALORIES (13% FROM FAT)
FAT 4.2G (SATURATED FAT 0.9G)
PROTEIN 20.6G CARBOHYDRATE 39.6G
CHOLESTEROL 49MG SODIUM 531MG

White Chili

(pictured on page 127)

1 cup dried navy beans
3 (10½-ounce) cans ready-to-serve, no-salt-added chicken broth
1 cup water
1¼ cups chopped onion
1 clove garlic, minced
¼ teaspoon salt
2 cups chopped cooked chicken breasts (skinned before cooking and cooked without salt)
1 (4.5-ounce) can chopped green chiles
1 teaspoon ground cumin
¾ teaspoon dried oregano
¼ teaspoon ground red pepper
⅛ teaspoon ground cloves
¾ cup (3 ounces) shredded 40%-less-fat Monterey Jack cheese

Sort and wash beans; place in a Dutch oven. Cover with water 2 inches above beans; let soak 8 hours. Drain beans, and return to Dutch oven.

Add broth and next 4 ingredients to Dutch oven. Bring to a boil; cover, reduce heat, and simmer 2 hours, stirring occasionally.

Add chicken and next 5 ingredients; cover and cook 30 minutes. Spoon into serving bowls; top each with cheese. **Yield: 6 (1-cup) servings.**

PER SERVING: 269 CALORIES (17% FROM FAT)
FAT 5.2G (SATURATED FAT 2.3G)
PROTEIN 26.2G CARBOHYDRATE 27.7G
CHOLESTEROL 46MG SODIUM 304MG

Defat Chicken Broth

To defat commercial chicken broth, place the unopened can in the refrigerator at least 1 hour before using. Open the can, and skim off the layer of solidified fat.

South-of-the-Border Chili

1 pound lean boneless top round steak,
    trimmed
Vegetable cooking spray
½ cup chopped onion
1 clove garlic, minced
2 tablespoons chili powder
1 tablespoon cocoa
1 teaspoon dried oregano
½ teaspoon salt
½ teaspoon ground cumin
1 (8-ounce) can no-salt-added tomato sauce
2 cups water
2 cups hot cooked rice (cooked without salt
    or fat)

Partially freeze top round steak; cut into ½-inch cubes, and set aside.

Coat a Dutch oven with cooking spray; place over medium-high heat until hot. Add onion and garlic; cook until tender, stirring constantly.

Add meat, and cook until meat browns, stirring often. Stir in chili powder and next 6 ingredients; bring to a boil.

Cover, reduce heat, and simmer 1 hour, stirring often. Serve over rice. **Yield: 4 (¾-cup) servings.**

PER SERVING: 314 CALORIES (17% FROM FAT)
FAT 5.8G (SATURATED FAT 1.9G)
PROTEIN 29.7G CARBOHYDRATE 34.5G
CHOLESTEROL 65MG SODIUM 404MG

Lower the Fat

For the health-conscious, ground chuck, top round, and venison are good lean choices for chili. Ground or chopped chicken or turkey breast may replace red meat in many recipes.

Hot Venison Chili

2 pounds lean venison stew meat, diced
1 tablespoon olive oil
1¾ cups chopped onion
1 cup diced celery
3 cloves garlic, crushed
3 cups water
3 (14½-ounce) cans no-salt-added tomatoes,
    undrained and chopped
2 (10-ounce) cans diced tomatoes with green
    chiles, undrained
2 tablespoons chili powder
1½ tablespoons reduced-sodium
    Worcestershire sauce
¼ teaspoon dried thyme
¼ teaspoon dried oregano
¼ teaspoon ground cumin
¼ teaspoon salt
1 (16-ounce) can no-salt-added kidney beans,
    undrained
2 cups finely shredded iceberg lettuce
½ cup (2 ounces) shredded reduced-fat sharp
    Cheddar cheese
½ cup diced tomato

Brown venison in hot oil in a Dutch oven, stirring constantly. Stir in onion, celery, and garlic; cook until tender.

Add water and next 8 ingredients; bring to a boil. Reduce heat, and simmer, uncovered, 2 hours, stirring occasionally. Add beans, and cook 30 minutes.

Ladle chili into individual bowls. Top each serving with ¼ cup lettuce, 1 tablespoon cheese, and 1 tablespoon tomato. **Yield: 8 (1½-cup) servings.**

PER SERVING: 287 CALORIES (20% FROM FAT)
FAT 6.4G (SATURATED FAT 2.2G)
PROTEIN 33.6G CARBOHYDRATE 23.9G
CHOLESTEROL 101MG SODIUM 289MG

From top: South-of-the-Border Chili, White Chili (page 125), and Hot Venison Chili

Healthy Heroes

¾ cup thinly sliced fresh mushrooms
½ cup seeded and chopped cucumber
1 tablespoon sliced green onions
1 clove garlic, minced
2 tablespoons balsamic vinegar
⅛ teaspoon freshly ground pepper
1 (2-ounce) hoagie bun
2 lettuce leaves
2 ounces thinly sliced lean ham
2 ounces thinly sliced turkey breast
4 slices tomato
¼ cup (1 ounce) shredded part-skim
    mozzarella cheese

Combine first 6 ingredients in a small bowl; let mixture stand 30 minutes.

Slice bun in half lengthwise; pull out soft inside of top and bottom, leaving a shell (reserve crumbs for another use).

Spoon mushroom mixture into each half of bun; cover with a lettuce leaf. Top with ham, turkey, tomato, and cheese. Cut in half to serve.
Yield: 2 servings.

PER SERVING: 206 CALORIES (29% FROM FAT)
FAT 6.6G (SATURATED FAT 3.0G)
PROTEIN 20.2G CARBOHYDRATE 16.0G
CHOLESTEROL 52MG SODIUM 546MG

128   Soups and Sandwiches

Open-Faced Breakfast Sandwiches

½ cup light process cream cheese
4 whole wheat English muffins, split and
    toasted
½ cup low-sugar orange marmalade
8 (1-ounce) slices lean Canadian bacon
1 cup alfalfa sprouts
32 mandarin orange segments

Spread 1 tablespoon cream cheese on cut side of each muffin half; spread 1 tablespoon orange marmalade over cream cheese. Top with Canadian bacon; place on a baking sheet.

Broil 5 inches from heat (with electric oven door partially opened) 3 minutes or until hot. Remove from oven; top each with 2 tablespoons alfalfa sprouts and 4 orange segments. Serve immediately. **Yield: 8 servings.**

PER SERVING: 171 CALORIES (26% FROM FAT)
FAT 5.0G (SATURATED FAT 2.3G)
PROTEIN 10.2G CARBOHYDRATE 20.8G
CHOLESTEROL 22MG SODIUM 650MG

Turkey-in-the-Slaw Sandwich

1 cup shredded green cabbage
1 cup shredded red cabbage
½ cup shredded carrot
¼ cup reduced-calorie mayonnaise
¼ cup plain nonfat yogurt
1½ teaspoons sugar
¼ teaspoon ground white pepper
8 slices whole wheat bread
1 tablespoon commercial reduced-calorie
    Thousand Island salad dressing
¾ pound thinly sliced cooked turkey

Combine first 7 ingredients in a large bowl; cover and chill.

Spread 4 slices of bread equally with dressing. Place 3 ounces sliced turkey and one-fourth of slaw on each slice of bread; top with remaining bread slices. Cut each sandwich in half, and secure with wooden picks. **Yield: 4 servings.**

PER SERVING: 330 CALORIES (24% FROM FAT)
FAT 8.8G (SATURATED FAT 1.8G)
PROTEIN 32.1G CARBOHYDRATE 31.6G
CHOLESTEROL 66MG SODIUM 488MG

Smoked Turkey-Roasted Pepper Sandwiches

2 tablespoons nonfat cream cheese, softened
1 tablespoon reduced-fat mayonnaise
1 tablespoon spicy brown mustard
⅛ teaspoon pepper
¼ cup chopped commercial roasted red
    peppers, drained
2 tablespoons sliced green onions
8 slices pumpernickel bread
¾ pound sliced smoked turkey breast
¼ cup alfalfa sprouts

Combine first 4 ingredients; stir in red peppers and green onions.

Spread mixture evenly on one side of bread slices. Layer turkey and alfalfa sprouts on 4 slices of bread; top with remaining bread slices. Cut each sandwich in half.

Serve immediately, or wrap each sandwich in heavy-duty plastic wrap and refrigerate. **Yield: 4 servings.**

Note: Smoked turkey breast is soaked in a salt solution before smoking, increasing its sodium content. If you're watching your sodium, substitute roasted turkey breast for the smoked.

PER SERVING: 280 CALORIES (9% FROM FAT)
FAT 2.9G (SATURATED FAT 0.1G)
PROTEIN 29.1G CARBOHYDRATE 36.3G
CHOLESTEROL 44MG SODIUM 1057MG

Fiesta Burgers

hamburger patty, 2 tablespoons tomato mixture, and top half of bun. **Yield: 8 servings.**

Salmon Burgers

1 (15-ounce) can pink salmon, undrained
1 large egg, lightly beaten
½ cup unsalted saltine cracker crumbs
¼ cup finely chopped onion
¼ cup finely chopped celery
½ teaspoon baking powder
Vegetable cooking spray
½ cup nonfat mayonnaise
2 tablespoons lemon juice
½ teaspoon dried dillweed
¼ teaspoon pepper
¼ teaspoon hot sauce
6 onion sandwich rolls, split
6 tomato slices
1 cup shredded lettuce

   Drain salmon, reserving liquid; remove and discard skin and bones. Flake salmon with a fork.
   Combine salmon and next 5 ingredients. Add 1 to 2 tablespoons reserved liquid, stirring until mixture sticks together. Shape into 6 patties; set aside.
   Coat a large nonstick skillet with cooking spray; add salmon patties, and cook over medium heat about 4 minutes on each side or until lightly browned. Keep warm.
   Combine mayonnaise and next 4 ingredients; spread on cut sides of rolls. Place a salmon patty on bottom half of each roll; top each with a tomato slice, lettuce, and top half of bun. **Yield: 6 servings.**

Fiesta Burgers

1⅓ cups seeded, chopped unpeeled tomato
¼ cup finely chopped onion
¼ cup taco sauce
1 (4.5-ounce) can chopped green chiles, drained
2 pounds 93% or 96% low-fat ground beef
2 tablespoons Worcestershire sauce
½ teaspoon ground cumin
¼ teaspoon onion powder
¼ teaspoon garlic powder
Vegetable cooking spray
8 (1½-ounce) hamburger buns
8 lettuce leaves

   Combine first 4 ingredients in a bowl; cover and chill 30 minutes.
   Combine beef and next 4 ingredients; divide into 8 equal portions, shaping each into a ½-inch-thick patty. Place on rack of a broiler pan coated with cooking spray.
   Broil 4 inches from heat (with electric oven door partially opened) 8 minutes on each side. Line bottom half of buns with a lettuce leaf; top each with 2 tablespoons tomato mixture, a

Vegetables

Indulge in the crisp textures and bright colors of these
favorite vegetables—all cooked in light ways
to preserve nutrients and flavors.

Southern-Style Creamed Corn, Oven-Fried Okra, Lemon Broccoli

Butterbeans, Parmesan-Stuffed Tomatoes, Grilled Sweet Potatoes, Pretty Pepper Kabobs

Roasted Red Pepper Corn, Italian Green Beans, Fresh Corn Pudding, Black-Eyed Peas

Herbed Tomato Slices, Stuffed Vidalia Onions, Oven French Fries

From front: Herbed Potatoes (page 137), Honey Rutabaga (page 139),
Braised Turnips (page 140), and Rosemary Carrots (page 133)

Butterbeans

Lemon Broccoli

2 tablespoons grated lemon rind
¼ teaspoon salt
¼ teaspoon freshly ground pepper
1½ pounds fresh broccoli
2 tablespoons lemon juice

Combine first 3 ingredients; set aside.
Remove broccoli leaves, and discard tough ends of stalks; cut into spears.
Arrange broccoli in a steamer basket over boiling water. Cover and steam 5 minutes or until crisp-tender.
Arrange broccoli on a serving platter. Sprinkle with lemon rind mixture and lemon juice. **Yield: 6 servings.**

PER SERVING: 33 CALORIES (11% FROM FAT)
FAT 0.4G (SATURATED FAT 0.0G)
PROTEIN 3.4G CARBOHYDRATE 6.7G
CHOLESTEROL 0MG SODIUM 128MG

Butterbeans

2 cups water
1 ounce chopped lean ham
2 cups shelled fresh butterbeans or lima beans
    (about 1¾ pounds)
¼ teaspoon salt
⅛ teaspoon pepper

Combine water and ham in a saucepan; bring to a boil, and cook 5 to 10 minutes. Add beans, salt, and pepper; bring to a boil.
Cover, reduce heat, and simmer 45 minutes or until beans are tender. **Yield: 4 (½-cup) servings.**

PER SERVING: 104 CALORIES (16% FROM FAT)
FAT 1.8G (SATURATED FAT 0.3G)
PROTEIN 6.5G CARBOHYDRATE 16.0G
CHOLESTEROL 4MG SODIUM 247MG

Roasted Red Pepper Corn

4 medium ears fresh corn
Butter-flavored cooking spray
¼ cup diced sweet red pepper

Remove husks and silks from corn. Place each ear on a piece of heavy-duty aluminum foil, and coat with cooking spray. Sprinkle 1 tablespoon sweet red pepper on each ear of corn.
Roll foil lengthwise around corn, and twist foil at each end. Bake at 500° for 20 minutes. **Yield: 4 servings.**

PER SERVING: 87 CALORIES (14% FROM FAT)
FAT 1.4G (SATURATED FAT 0.2G)
PROTEIN 2.5G CARBOHYDRATE 19.3G
CHOLESTEROL 0MG SODIUM 13MG

Rosemary Carrots

(pictured on page 131)

2¼ cups thinly sliced carrots
½ cup water
1 tablespoon brown sugar
1 tablespoon chopped chives
1 teaspoon chicken-flavored bouillon granules
½ teaspoon fresh rosemary
⅛ teaspoon pepper

Combine carrots and water in a saucepan; bring to a boil. Cover, reduce heat, and simmer 7 minutes or until carrots are crisp-tender. Drain, reserving 2 tablespoons liquid.

Combine reserved liquid, brown sugar, and remaining ingredients in a saucepan.

Bring mixture to a boil over medium heat, stirring constantly; pour over carrots and toss. **Yield: 4 (½-cup) servings.**

PER SERVING: 38 CALORIES (9% FROM FAT)
FAT 0.4G (SATURATED FAT 0.1G)
PROTEIN 0.8G CARBOHYDRATE 8.7G
CHOLESTEROL 0MG SODIUM 227MG

Italian Green Beans

Italian Green Beans

1 pound fresh green beans
1 medium onion, sliced and separated into rings
3 cloves garlic
1 teaspoon vegetable oil
2 tablespoons water
1 teaspoon sugar
1 teaspoon dried basil
¼ teaspoon salt
2 tablespoons grated Parmesan cheese

Wash green beans; trim ends, and remove strings.

Add water to depth of 1 inch in a large skillet; bring to a boil, and add beans. Cover, reduce heat, and cook 6 to 8 minutes. Drain and immediately place in ice water. Let stand 5 minutes; drain well.

Cook onion and garlic in oil in a large skillet over medium-high heat, stirring constantly, until tender. Add green beans; cook 1 minute, stirring constantly.

Add 2 tablespoons water, sugar, basil, and salt; cook 1 to 2 minutes, stirring constantly. Remove and discard garlic; sprinkle with Parmesan cheese. **Yield: 3 (1-cup) servings.**

PER SERVING: 98 CALORIES (26% FROM FAT)
FAT 2.8G (SATURATED FAT 1.0G)
PROTEIN 4.6G CARBOHYDRATE 16.2G
CHOLESTEROL 3MG SODIUM 267MG

Cooking Vegetables

The most nutritious vegetables are those that aren't overcooked. Steaming, stir-frying, sautéing, and grilling are great ways to cook vegetables to bring out their natural flavors. Try adding herbs or spices to further enhance the taste.

Fresh Corn Pudding

Southern-Style Creamed Corn

6 medium ears fresh corn
1 cup 1% low-fat milk, divided
2 teaspoons cornstarch
2 (½-inch thick) onion slices
¼ teaspoon salt
¼ teaspoon ground white or black pepper

Cut off tips of kernels into a large bowl; scrape milk and remaining pulp from cob, using a small paring knife. Set aside.

Combine ¼ cup milk and cornstarch; set mixture aside.

Combine remaining ¾ cup milk and onion in a heavy saucepan; bring to a boil over medium heat. Cover, reduce heat, and simmer 5 minutes; remove and discard onion.

Add corn; cook over medium heat, stirring frequently, 5 minutes. Gradually stir in cornstarch mixture, salt, and pepper. Cook, stirring constantly, until thickened and bubbly (about 3 minutes). **Yield: 6 (½-cup) servings.**

PER SERVING: 103 CALORIES (12% FROM FAT)
FAT 1.4G (SATURATED FAT 0.4G)
PROTEIN 3.8G CARBOHYDRATE 22.0G
CHOLESTEROL 2MG SODIUM 131MG

Fresh Corn Pudding

2 cups corn cut from cob (about 4 medium ears)
1 tablespoon minced green pepper
1½ tablespoons all-purpose flour
2 teaspoons sugar
¼ teaspoon salt
¼ teaspoon mace
Dash of ground red pepper
½ cup egg substitute
1 cup evaporated skimmed milk
Vegetable cooking spray

Combine first 7 ingredients, stirring well. Combine egg substitute and evaporated milk; add to corn mixture.

Spoon mixture into a 1-quart baking dish coated with cooking spray. Place dish in a large shallow pan; add water to pan to a depth of 1 inch.

Bake at 350° for 1 hour or until a knife inserted in center comes out clean. **Yield: 6 (½-cup) servings.**

PER SERVING: 102 CALORIES (7% FROM FAT)
FAT 0.8G (SATURATED FAT 0.2G)
PROTEIN 7.1G CARBOHYDRATE 18.0G
CHOLESTEROL 2MG SODIUM 185MG

Stuffed Vidalia Onions

(pictured on page 140)

4 medium Vidalia onions (about 1½ pounds)
2 tablespoons oil-free Italian dressing
½ cup diced sweet red pepper
1 cup diced zucchini
½ cup soft breadcrumbs
½ cup (2 ounces) shredded part-skim
    mozzarella cheese
2 tablespoons minced fresh parsley
¼ teaspoon dried oregano
Dash of hot sauce
Vegetable cooking spray
Garnishes: paprika, fresh parsley sprigs

Peel onions, and cut a slice from top and bottom; chop slices, and set aside.

Cook onions in boiling water 15 to 20 minutes or until tender but not mushy. Cool. Remove center of onions, leaving shells intact; reserve onion centers for another use. Set onion shells aside.

Heat Italian dressing in a medium skillet until hot; add chopped onion, red pepper, and zucchini, and cook until tender, stirring constantly. Remove from heat; stir in breadcrumbs and next 4 ingredients.

Fill each onion shell with ½ cup vegetable mixture; place filled shells in an 8-inch square

baking dish coated with cooking spray.

Cover and bake at 350° for 20 minutes. Uncover and bake 5 additional minutes. Garnish, if desired. **Yield: 4 servings.**

PER SERVING: 111 CALORIES (24% FROM FAT)
FAT 3.0G (SATURATED FAT 1.5G)
PROTEIN 5.9G CARBOHYDRATE 16.2G
CHOLESTEROL 8MG SODIUM 182MG

Oven-Fried Okra

1 pound fresh okra
¼ cup egg substitute
¼ cup nonfat buttermilk
⅔ cup cornmeal
⅓ cup all-purpose flour
1 teaspoon baking powder
½ teaspoon salt
1 tablespoon vegetable oil
Vegetable cooking spray

Wash okra and drain. Remove tips and stem ends; cut okra crosswise into ½-inch slices.

Combine egg substitute and buttermilk; add okra, stirring to coat well. Let stand 10 minutes.

Combine cornmeal and next 3 ingredients in a zip-top plastic bag. Drain okra, small portions at a time, using a slotted spoon; place okra in bag with cornmeal mixture, shaking gently to coat.

Brush oil on a 15- x 10- x 1-inch jellyroll pan; add okra in a single layer.

Coat okra with cooking spray, and bake at 450° for 8 minutes. Stir well, and spray with cooking spray again; bake 7 to 8 additional minutes. After last baking, broil 4 inches from heat (with electric oven door partially opened) 4 to 5 minutes or until browned, stirring occasionally. **Yield: 7 (½-cup) servings.**

PER SERVING: 113 CALORIES (23% FROM FAT)
FAT 2.9G (SATURATED FAT 0.5G)
PROTEIN 3.9G CARBOHYDRATE 18.6G
CHOLESTEROL 0MG SODIUM 198MG

Black-Eyed Peas

Black-Eyed Peas

6 cups fresh black-eyed peas
3 (14½-ounce) cans ready-to-serve, reduced-
  sodium, fat-free chicken broth
2 teaspoons Creole seasoning
1 teaspoon olive oil
¼ teaspoon hot sauce

Combine all ingredients in a Dutch oven;
bring to a boil. Cover, reduce heat, and simmer
45 minutes or until tender, stirring occasionally.
Serve with a slotted spoon. **Yield: 6 (1-cup)
servings.**

Note: 2 (16-ounce) packages frozen black-
eyed peas may be substituted for 6 cups fresh
black-eyed peas.

PER SERVING: 259 CALORIES (11% FROM FAT)
FAT 3.1G (SATURATED FAT 0.4G)
PROTEIN 16.5G CARBOHYDRATE 42.7G
CHOLESTEROL 0MG SODIUM 193MG

Deviled Purple Hull Peas

3 cups shelled fresh purple hull peas or
  black-eyed peas (1 pound)
2 cups water
½ teaspoon salt
2 tablespoons cider vinegar
1 teaspoon dry mustard
¼ teaspoon sugar
¼ teaspoon pepper
1 clove garlic, minced
1 tablespoon chopped fresh parsley

Combine first 3 ingredients in a large saucepan; bring to a boil. Cover, reduce heat, and simmer 30 minutes or until tender; drain, reserving
½ cup liquid.

Combine reserved liquid, vinegar, and next 4
ingredients in saucepan. Add peas, and cook, stirring occasionally, over medium heat 5 minutes or
until thoroughly heated. Spoon into a serving
bowl; top with parsley. **Yield: 6 (½-cup) servings.**

PER SERVING: 115 CALORIES (5% FROM FAT)
FAT 0.6G (SATURATED FAT 0.2G)
PROTEIN 7.3G CARBOHYDRATE 20.9G
CHOLESTEROL 0MG SODIUM 201MG

Pretty Pepper Kabobs

12 (6-inch) wooden skewers
1 large onion, cut into wedges
1 large sweet yellow pepper, cubed
1 large sweet red pepper, cubed
1 large green pepper, cubed
Olive oil-flavored cooking spray

Soak wooden skewers in water at least 30
minutes.

Alternate vegetables on skewers; spray each
kabob with cooking spray.

Cook, covered with grill lid, over medium-hot
coals (350° to 400°) 8 to 10 minutes or until
done, turning frequently. **Yield: 8 servings.**

PER SERVING: 22 CALORIES (20% FROM FAT)
FAT 0.5G (SATURATED FAT 0.0G)
PROTEIN 0.7G CARBOHYDRATE 4.5G
CHOLESTEROL 0MG SODIUM 2MG

Grilled Sweet Potatoes

2 pounds sweet potatoes, peeled and cut into
    wedges
3 tablespoons reduced-sodium soy sauce
2 tablespoons dry sherry
2 tablespoons honey
2 tablespoons water
1 clove garlic, minced
Vegetable cooking spray
1 tablespoon sesame oil

Arrange sweet potato in a steamer basket; place over boiling water. Cover and steam 5 to 7 minutes.

Combine soy sauce and next 4 ingredients in a shallow dish; add sweet potato, and toss gently.

Drain sweet potato, reserving soy sauce mixture. Arrange sweet potato in a single layer in a grill basket coated with cooking spray; brush wedges with sesame oil.

Cook, covered with grill lid, over medium coals (300° to 350°) 15 minutes, basting with reserved soy sauce mixture and turning several times. **Yield: 6 servings.**

PER SERVING: 167 CALORIES (15% FROM FAT)
FAT 2.7G (SATURATED FAT 0.4G)
PROTEIN 2.3G CARBOHYDRATE 34.3G
CHOLESTEROL 0MG SODIUM 257MG

Oven French Fries

½ cup grated Parmesan cheese
2 teaspoons dried oregano
2 (8-ounce) baking potatoes, unpeeled
1 egg white, beaten
Vegetable cooking spray

Combine Parmesan cheese and oregano, and set aside.

Cut each potato lengthwise into 8 wedges; dip wedges into egg white, and dredge in Parmesan cheese mixture.

Place fries on a baking sheet coated with cooking spray. Bake at 425° for 25 minutes. **Yield: 4 (4-wedge) servings.**

PER SERVING: 137 CALORIES (22% FROM FAT)
FAT 3.4G (SATURATED FAT 2.0G)
PROTEIN 7.6G CARBOHYDRATE 19.8G
CHOLESTEROL 8MG SODIUM 207MG

Herbed Potatoes

(pictured on page 131)

Vegetable cooking spray
4 medium baking potatoes, cut into ¼-inch
    slices (1½ pounds)
2 medium-size white onions, cut into ¼-inch
    slices (12 ounces)
5 plum tomatoes, sliced (1 pound)
½ teaspoon salt
1 teaspoon dried thyme
¾ teaspoon dried rosemary, crushed
1 tablespoon olive oil
2 tablespoons chopped fresh parsley

Coat a 13- x 9- x 2-inch baking dish with cooking spray. Layer half each of potato, onion, and tomato in dish; sprinkle with half each of salt, thyme, and rosemary. Repeat layers, and drizzle evenly with olive oil.

Cover and bake at 425° for 35 to 40 minutes or until tender. Sprinkle with parsley. **Yield: 8 (¾-cup) servings.**

PER SERVING: 108 CALORIES (18% FROM FAT)
FAT 2.1G (SATURATED FAT 0.3G)
PROTEIN 2.9G CARBOHYDRATE 20.7G
CHOLESTEROL 0MG SODIUM 159MG

Mexican-Stuffed Potatoes

Mexican-Stuffed Potatoes

4 medium baking potatoes (1½ pounds)
1 (8-ounce) carton plain low-fat yogurt
¼ cup skim milk
⅛ teaspoon pepper
1 (4.5-ounce) can chopped green chiles,
    drained
1 (2-ounce) jar diced pimiento, drained
4 large, pitted ripe olives, chopped
½ cup (2 ounces) shredded 40%-less-fat
    sharp Cheddar cheese, divided

Wash potatoes; prick several times with a
fork. Bake at 400° for 1 hour or until done. Let
cool to touch. Cut potatoes in half lengthwise;
carefully scoop out pulp, leaving shells intact.
Set aside.
  Combine potato pulp, yogurt, milk, and pepper; mash until light and fluffy.
  Stir chiles, pimiento, olives, and half of
Cheddar cheese into potato mixture. Stuff shells
with potato mixture; place on an ungreased baking sheet.
  Bake at 375° for 10 minutes. Sprinkle evenly
with remaining cheese, and bake 2 additional
minutes. **Yield: 8 servings.**

PER SERVING: 111 CALORIES (17% FROM FAT)
FAT 2.1G (SATURATED FAT 1.1G)
PROTEIN 5.9G CARBOHYDRATE 17.9G
CHOLESTEROL 7MG SODIUM 136MG

Honey Rutabaga

(pictured on page 131)

½ cup dry white wine
1 tablespoon brown sugar
2 tablespoons honey
2 teaspoons reduced-calorie margarine
4 cups cubed, uncooked rutabaga

Combine all ingredients in a large saucepan.
Bring to a boil; cover, reduce heat, and simmer
40 to 45 minutes. **Yield: 5 (¾-cup) servings.**

PER SERVING: 82 CALORIES (13% FROM FAT)
FAT 1.2G (SATURATED FAT 0.2G)
PROTEIN 1.4G CARBOHYDRATE 18.2G
CHOLESTEROL 0MG SODIUM 40MG

Parmesan-Stuffed Tomatoes

(pictured on page 111)

4 medium tomatoes (2½ pounds)
3 tablespoons chopped green onions
2 tablespoons chopped green pepper
1 teaspoon reduced-calorie margarine, melted
¼ cup Italian-seasoned breadcrumbs
2 tablespoons chopped fresh parsley
⅛ teaspoon dried oregano
⅛ teaspoon ground red pepper
⅛ teaspoon black pepper
Vegetable cooking spray
2 tablespoons grated Parmesan cheese

Slice off top of each tomato, and carefully
scoop out pulp. Set tomato shells and pulp aside.
  Cook green onions and green pepper in margarine in a large skillet over medium-high heat,
stirring constantly, until tender. Remove from heat.
  Stir in tomato pulp, breadcrumbs, and next 4
ingredients. Spoon into shells, and place in an 8-
inch square baking dish coated with cooking spray.
  Cover and bake at 350° for 25 minutes.
Sprinkle with cheese, and broil 5 inches from
heat (with electric oven door partially opened) 3
minutes or until golden. **Yield: 4 servings.**

PER SERVING: 106 CALORIES (23% FROM FAT)
FAT 2.7G (SATURATED FAT 0.8G)
PROTEIN 4.6G CARBOHYDRATE 18.6G
CHOLESTEROL 2MG SODIUM 281MG

From left: Stuffed Vidalia Onions (page 135) and Herbed Tomato Slices

Herbed Tomato Slices

15 (½-inch-thick) tomato slices
Butter-flavored cooking spray
⅓ cup Italian-seasoned breadcrumbs
2 tablespoons grated Parmesan cheese
¾ teaspoon finely chopped fresh basil or
   ¼ teaspoon dried basil
Garnish: fresh basil sprigs

Arrange tomato slices in a 13- x 9- x 2-inch baking dish coated with cooking spray; coat tomato slices with cooking spray. Set aside.

Combine breadcrumbs, cheese, and chopped basil; sprinkle evenly over tomato slices. Bake at 350° for 15 to 20 minutes. Garnish, if desired. **Yield: 5 servings.**

PER SERVING: 48 CALORIES (23% FROM FAT)
FAT 1.2G (SATURATED FAT 0.5G)
PROTEIN 2.3G CARBOHYDRATE 7.4G
CHOLESTEROL 2MG SODIUM 248MG

Braised Turnips

(pictured on page 131)

1 tablespoon reduced-calorie margarine
5 cups julienne-sliced turnips
1 tablespoon sugar
⅛ teaspoon salt
⅓ cup ready-to-serve, no-salt-added chicken
   broth
3 tablespoons chopped fresh parsley
1 tablespoon lemon juice

Combine first 4 ingredients in a nonstick skillet; cook over low heat 8 to 10 minutes, stirring occasionally.

Stir in broth, parsley, and lemon juice; cover and cook over low heat 5 to 7 minutes or until tender. **Yield: 7 (½-cup) servings.**

PER SERVING: 42 CALORIES (24% FROM FAT)
FAT 1.1G (SATURATED FAT 0.2G)
PROTEIN 0.8G CARBOHYDRATE 7.8G
CHOLESTEROL 0MG SODIUM 120MG

Index